'Black **Lies** Matter'

Copyright 2016

Taleeb Starkes

The news headlines referenced throughout this book are actual, unadulterated, headlines. In many instances, my comments are noted underneath the headlines **[in bold parentheses]** to emphasize a point. Read the e-book for hyperlinked headlines and sources.

Eternal gratitude to Claire "The Saint" Hawksley. I threw a Hail Mary pass and you leaped higher than anyone else to catch it... You're truly a godsend.

Foreword
Trigger Warning

WHY TALEEB?

In 2011, when Ann Coulter told Sean Hannity, *"Our blacks are so much better than their blacks,"* the mainstream media went nuts. Whoopi Goldberg said, *"I didn't know we were anybody's blacks,"* and even right wing news sources were informing Ann that slavery had been abolished. They were all being willfully ignorant because we are so desperate for racist villains, we'll lynch anyone who talks openly about race. Ann was clearly referring to Herman Cain, and everyone ignored the second half of her quote where she added, *"You have fought against probably your family, probably your neighbors. . . that's why we have very impressive blacks."* She was speaking about African-American people of color (or whatever the term is this week) who have the courage to be truthful and blunt no matter how uncomfortable it makes their fellow blacks feel.

Half a century ago, we had the Freedom Riders daring to go town to town in the South commingling with blacks in areas where such actions were verboten. Today, the courageous ones are on the right. When Ann says *"our"* she's talking about the likes of Thomas Sowell, Deroy Murdock, Jason Riley, and Allen West. These black men brave family gatherings such as Thanksgiving and confront their family members with counterintuitive thoughts like, *"welfare is bad for the black family"* and *"legal guns make bad neighborhoods safer."* This is not how liberals want blacks to behave. Blacks are meant to push for social programs and vote Democrat even though the Dems have caused them nothing but trouble since the Civil Rights Act. Liberals demand blacks vote for gay marriage even if that contradicts their religious beliefs. If ex-KKK member David Duke likes Trump, we have to gasp in horror but if ex-KKK member and Democrat Robert Byrd endorses Hillary and Obama, we're meant to ignore it. Liberals push Planned Parenthood on the hood even though abortions have killed more blacks than, well, anything. The left treats blacks like whimpering pets they can trot out in commercials to gain more votes, taxes, and power. The right wants to treat them as adults.

When I think of *"our blacks,"* I cast a wider net than Ann. *"Our"* refers to those of us brave enough to champion free speech and tell it like it is no matter how much it hurts. We speak on the record the way we all talk in bars. *"Our"* is the people in the trenches, willing to make the tough decisions no matter how unpopular it makes them. The aforementioned conservative black intellectuals are great, but they're also nerds. I'm a fan of conservative blacks who possess an urban veneer. I'm talking about the likes of Sonnie Johnson, and yes, Taleeb Starkes. Thomas Sowell lives in a beautiful mansion in sunny California. Starkes lives in a modest row home in Philly. Where many of the conservative blacks Ann was referring to make their living pontificating about a history they left behind, Taleeb is in it. His full-time job is working with troubled teens who don't fit into the system. They challenge him to fist fights and he has to constantly juggle not losing face with not losing his job. I'm more apt to listen to Taleeb's views on poor, black teenagers or, as the media call them, *"youths."* It's easy to come up with solutions for the worst of the worst sitting at your desk, but Taleeb's answer is shocking. *"Remove the weeds from the garden,"* he says of the irreparable few, *"Separate the liabilities from the assets."* While many can be whipped into shape and encouraged to assimilate, there are plenty who are *"disrespected"* because they haven't earned respect.

This is the kind of voice needed moving forward in America, someone who's actually been there. When we listen to the people in the trenches such as Starkes, we all prosper. He's rough around the edges and so blatantly honest, it makes most of us uncomfortable. He's not an academic and doesn't use pretentious verbiage. Moreover, his books explain what is really going on in America in a language that the people most affected by it can understand. In that sense, there is no voice more relevant than Taleeb's. These are not hypothetical scenarios. This is the truth.

Gavin McInnes
Co-Founder, *VICE Media*
Founder, *StreetCarnage.com*
Host, *The Gavin McInnes Show*

* * *

"If you want truth to go round the world you must hire an express train to pull it; but if you want a lie to go round the world, it will fly; it is as light as a feather, and a breath will carry it. It is well said in the old Proverb, 'A lie will go round the world while truth is pulling its boots on.'"

- Charles Haddon Spurgeon

Table of Contents

Chapter I

The Race Grievance Industry

"White America is a syndicate arrayed to protect its exclusive power to dominate and control our bodies. Sometimes this power is direct (lynching), and sometimes it is insidious (redlining)."
— Ta-Nehisi Coates

Have you noticed the unchanged pattern of outrage that manifests from the black community whenever a black life is taken by a white person, especially a white cop? Also, have you noticed that the same culture-vultures arrive without hesitation to gluttonously feast during these incidents? They figuratively pick apart the black body until it's a carcass — leaving nothing for bacteria to decompose. These opportunists are arsonists dressed as first responders, and their mission is to start racial infernos. In other words, they racialize not harmonize.

Undoubtedly, you've noticed this trend — even if you're a bleeding-heart liberal.

One must understand that these "call to action" reactions are not spontaneous. They're calculated maneuvers promoted by an ever-present Race Grievance Industry (RGI), an industry whose only product is victimhood — and it's manufactured without pause.

The RGI's sole purpose is to profit from racial strife under the guise of pursuing racial peace. Its modus operandi is rooted in a lie that refuses to die: blacks are permanent victims of racism and no amount of effort will overcome it. The lie is rinsed and repeated in different ways, but the message remains unchanged — America is a racist labyrinth specifically designed to stifle black advancement.

A century ago, Booker T. Washington noticed the RGI's agenda:

"There is another class of coloured people who make a business of keeping the troubles, the wrongs, and the hardships of the Negro race before the public. Having learned that they are able to make a living out of their troubles, they have grown into the settled habit of advertising their wrongs — partly because they want sympathy and partly because it pays. Some of these people do not want the Negro to lose his grievances, because they do not want to lose their jobs.[1]"

On one hand, the RGI will declare that race is a social construct, but then use race to socially construct a paycheck. Even when blacks are the majority population in cities such as Baltimore, and occupy key positions — mayor, city council, city council president, police chief, fire chief, school superintendent, etc. — the RGI still schemes to convince blacks that racism is America's default setting. Food for thought: If a city that had a predominantly gay populace, gay mayor, gay city council with a gay president, gay police chief, and gay fire chief, etc. blamed homophobia for its problems, wouldn't that be laughable? By the way, I hope the Gaystapo don't come after me for that analogy.

NY State Senators wore Hoodies to the State Capital

RGI's Theory of Exploitivity

Regardless of evidence, circumstances, or facts, the RGI's predictable scavenger hunt that summarily ensues after any unfortunate white-on-black incident stems from what I've termed... the "Theory of Exploitivity."

The Theory of Exploitivity declares racism as the motive for any disagreeable white-on-black incident. Racism is the end-all-be-all explanation: no fact finding mission is necessary. Moreover, this one-dimensional, race-based concept is unapologetically absolute with no room for debate. In simple terms, the Theory of Exploitivity translates as *Black Victim + White Culprit = Racism*. And, due to the theory's continued success for the RGI, so-called white Hispanics have now been included as White Culprits and thus, are eligible for exploitation. On the other hand, so-called black Hispanics don't fit the agenda (for obvious pigment-related reasons).

This time-tested equation of *Black Victim + White Culprit = Racism* has proven to be just as vital to the RGI as $E=mc^2$ was to Albert Einstein. And just as Einstein's Theory of Relativity has revolutionized science, the Theory of Exploitivity has revolutionized the science of victimology, while generating untold wealth for its practitioners. In fact, Al Sharpton, the RGI's most visible board member, routinely has more corporate sponsors for his events than colleges have for their bowl games.

Al "Shakedown" Sharpton

For years, "Shakedown" Sharpton — a former Federal Bureau of Investigation (FBI) informant[2] — has enriched himself by threatening companies with bad publicity if they didn't financially support his agenda. Judging from his body of work, he's the quintessential race hustler. Robert F. Kennedy Jr., a certified limousine-liberal, and political elite mainstay, once served a month-long stint in a Puerto Rican prison with Sharpton for trespassing. RFK Jr. wrote these scathing comments about "Shakedown" Sharpton in his diary:

"Al Sharpton has done more damage to the black cause than George Wallace [segregationist Alabama Governor]. He has suffocated the decent black leaders in New York," — "His transparent venal blackmail and extortion schemes taint all black leadership."

Diary bombshell: RFK's slams against Al Sharpton, Jesse Jackson and Gov. Cuomo
nypost.com

Whenever "Shakedown" Al needs sponsors for his annual National Action Network (NAN) — the civil rights group he founded and leads — conference, he licks his chops. *The New York Post* reported:

"Anheuser-Busch gave him six figures, Colgate-Palmolive shelled out $50,000 and Macy's and Pfizer have contributed thousands to the Rev. Al

Sharpton's charity. Almost 50 companies – including PepsiCo, General Motors, Wal-Mart, FedEx, Continental Airlines, Johnson & Johnson and Chase – and some labor unions sponsored Sharpton's National Action Network annual conference in April. Terrified of negative publicity, fearful of a consumer boycott or eager to make nice with the civil-rights activist, CEOs write checks, critics say, to NAN and Sharpton – who brandishes the buying power of African-American consumers. In some cases, they hire him as a consultant."

His NAN collected two million dollars more in 2014 than the prior year. Additionally, his pay increased from $241,545 in 2013 to $412,644, including a bonus of $64,400. Certainly, "Shakedown" Sharpton's extortion racket is the envy of other RGI members.

REV. AL SOAKS UP BOYCOTT BUCKS
nypost.com

Al Sharpton gives himself 71% raise thanks to de Blasio, Obama
nypost.com

Sharpton yells *"No justice, no peace"* while chasing the phantom menace of racism, but ignores the actual menaces that terrorize the community. Therefore, when it comes to resolving racial strife, I'd follow Caesar the Ape (from Planet of the Apes) before following Al the Hustler (from the Grievance Galaxy). After all, Caesar has a proven record of trustworthiness, and his integrity isn't financially incentivized.

Caesar > Al

RGI Members

Although the RGI has no official website, headquarters, or telephone number, its membership is an assorted bag of nuts from all races. They are everywhere yet nowhere that's needed. It mainly consists of blacks whose self-appointed profession is being black (pro-black for short), and these pro-blacks expect every black person to bleed red, black, and green, instead of red, white, and blue. Typically, the members are credentialed, influential, and successful — reverends, college professors, politicians, entertainers, television, and radio show hosts, athletes, et al — many living the American dream; yet dedicated to convincing black people that the American dream is a white privilege unattainable for blacks.

President Obama, who has no ancestral ties to enslaved Africans in America, occasionally contrives a pro-black image. However, the book *"Double Down: Game Change 2012"* revealed,

"Obama had little patience for the 'professional left,' and vanishingly close to zero for what one of his senior African American aides, Michael Strautmanis, referred to as 'professional blacks' (as opposed to black professionals)."

Tavis Smiley and Cornell West are running examples of Obama cold-shouldering some pro-blacks while tolerating others such as "Shakedown" Sharpton. Sharpton is still embraced because he gave Obama street credibility and refuses to publically criticize him. Overall, no one can stand the company of pro-blacks for long, not even other pro-blacks.

It shouldn't be surprising that the RGI also has non-black members, specifically white members. Contentedly seated behind the grievance-curtain are white liberals. Historically, white liberals have been the puppeteers of black movements while the foot soldiers were mostly non-white. The inconvenient truth is that most national black organizations need white support to start and grow. In fact, the original founders of the NAACP (National Association for the Advancement of Colored People) consisted of more whites than blacks. Of the NAACP's "Founding 8," Ida B. Wells and W.E.B. Dubois were the only blacks.

The NAACP's Founding 8

Having a white or even white-looking person as an ambassador of black causes is extremely beneficial to the RGI. Simply put, whites give black organizations credibility. Furthermore, having white or white-looking people as generals spreading the RGI's generalized lies makes general consumption easier. Presently, the head of the Congressional Black Caucus is G.W. Butterfield, a man who could easily pass as white but is black by a technicality (the "one-drop rule"). Shaun King[3], a Black Lives Matter aficionado who came to fame during the Ferguson fiasco of 2014, has a black belt in social justice jiu-jitsu but was exposed as a white guy passing as black. After being outed as a poser, his dedication to racial rabble-rousing has only intensified. Rachel Dolezal[4], a white woman who self-identified as a black woman, was once head of the NAACP's Spokane chapter; nothing could hold down that strong, black, independent woman except the white woman's body that housed her. Currently, she plans to write a book about people *"caught between boundary lines of race or culture or ethnicity."* I wonder if her book will also be white on the outside but black on the inside.

CBC Leader, BLM Leader, NAACP Leader, New Black Panther Party Leader?

White allies of the RGI beware. You are simply useful tools. Even after denouncing your white privilege to embrace white guilt, the unchangeable fact remains... you're white! White inner-city teachers can attest to the fact that being white equals being perpetually conscious of doing or saying anything that could be misinterpreted as "racist" — even though the teachers' worldview and career commitment to minorities prove otherwise.

Former media professor charged over 'siccing' muscle on student journalist during Mizzou protests says she was fired 'because she is white'
dailymail.co.uk

Last year, she was fighting for black students. This year, she's fighting for unemployment benefits

The RGI is the unofficial gatekeeper of black cultural identity, and its members don't deviate from the governing narrative of victimization. Regarding race matters, the members' opinions echo those of the collective; individual thought is shunned. The appearance of black racial unity takes precedence over addressing black pathologies. During the Zimmerman trial, a young and naive, newly sworn president of the NAACP's Norfolk, Virginia chapter learned the rules of the echo chamber. He audaciously posted on his private Facebook page that people should think logically and not racially over the case:

"As I look at this George Zimmerman case ... I wonder why is it that we are always willing to say someone who clearly had a shaky past, was the victim.' 'Are we blinded about why Trayvon was at his dad's house in the first place, and why he wasn't at home at the time he was shot? Please think logically and not racially..."

He had no idea that by pressing "enter" after the post, his time as NAACP president would become pressed. The RGI's thought-police were immediately summoned to muzzle this thought-fugitive. Local black officials called for his resignation, including Norfolk City Councilman Paul Riddick, who told WAVY-TV10, "*The national [NAACP] office should come into this. It would be an effort to silence this fellow. I don't know how recall process works, but I think they should recall him. He obviously does not have the maturity when to speak and when not to speak.*" The councilman added, "*My initial reaction, 'was that it wasn't true, that somebody had gone on his Facebook and had planted this.*" The ordeal meant that the young 25-year-old NAACP president had now been baptized by the Church of the Eternal Victim a.k.a the RGI.

'Think logically and not racially': Facebook message from NAACP chapter president about the Zimmerman trial brings calls for his resignation
dailymail.co.uk

Tristan Breaux
Fri at 11:39am •

As I look at this George Zimmerman case...I wonder why is it that we are always willing to say someone who clearly had a shaky past, was the victim. Are we blinded about why Trayvon was at his dads house in the first place, and why he wasnt at home at the time he was shot? Please think logically and not racially...

The post that almost cost him his NAACP post

RGI's Official Political Party

The Democrat party is the official party of the RGI, and it's due to the Democrats' overview of government as the savior. This belief perfectly suits the RGI's platform of victimization. As long as the Democrats continue to validate black victimhood, the RGI will ensure that blacks remain on the Democrat plantation. Because of this quid pro quo union, the two entities fit like hands in gloves.

The Democrat party and blacks fit tightly like O.J.'s gloves. Ahem..."alleged" gloves

It's no coincidence that cities with a predominantly black population are usually Democrat-controlled. And it's no coincidence that violence, dysfunction, and poverty are endemic in those places. Characteristically, the Democrat party prefers handouts to a hand up, and that's the reason it doesn't teach people how to fish; instead, it provides fish sticks. Yep, it's the party of fish sticks. In fact, the city council of majority-black-and Democrat-ruled Washington, D.C., unanimously approved a bill that included a proposal to pay residents a stipend not to commit crimes. Councilmember Kenyan McDuffie, a Democrat who wrote the legislation, said it was part of a comprehensive approach to reducing violent crime in the city, which experienced a 54 percent increase in homicides in 2015. *"I want to prevent violent crime — particularly gun violence — by addressing the root causes and creating opportunities for people, particularly those individuals who are at the highest risks of offending,"* wrote McDuffie in a letter to constituents. According to the District's independent chief financial officer, the program would cost taxpayers $4.9 million over four years, including $460,000 a year in stipend payments. In short, this is merely another Democrat-sponsored bailout for thugs. Remember, D.C. already possesses some of the strictest gun laws in the nation; yet, its 2015 homicide rate increased 54 percent from 2014[5]. Evidently, disarming law-abiding citizens hasn't deterred violent criminality. Consequently, the Democrats now want to take taxpayers' money to pay criminals not to victimize taxpayers who can't defend themselves because of D.C.'s gun ban. This Democrat tactic is nothing short of paying protection money to the mafia. Rewarding self-defeating behavior is another Democrat attribute that the RGI absolutely adores. I now understand why Democrat President Lyndon Johnson prophesized, *"I'll have those niggers voting Democrat for the next 200 years[6]."* Not only is his prophecy manifesting, but the *"two hundred years"* calculation might be short two hundred years.

DC bill would pay people stipends not to commit crimes
wtop.com

For black Democrat politicians, claims of racism have become legitimized as weapons to wield, or crutches to lean on. This option to invoke racism as the first and last line of defense enables black Democrat politicians to abuse their position and still maintain the support of many black constituents — even when their political indiscretions or outright crimes are undeniable. Black Republican politicians aren't extended the same luxury. For them, there's no supportive hammock from the black community, which is why being a black Republican politician is a brave but lonely endeavor. Consider ex-Detroit mayor Kwame Kilpatrick, a Democrat who — after pimping and prostituting the mayor's office for millions of dollars — was convicted of numerous crimes that severely affected "black" Detroit. Even so, his brother-in-law's statements about Kilpatrick's case reflected a credible sentiment felt by Kilpatrick's base. Here are a few quotes:

"You talk about race, come on man, that's what it is. If Kwame Kilpatrick was white and his name was Kent Masters Kensington, he would not be on trial."

"It's almost a travesty that they're even on trial. If you take a consensus of the people in the city... people would reelect [Kilpatrick] today. He would win right now, and there in my logic lies the travesty. I mean, here it is, they're trying to get people to hate the guy that they elected, and here it is 10 years later and the people still would vote him in office and they still champion him on his work. Now, the affair and all that other stuff, yeah, ok. But his body of work, you cannot question it."

"What happened here in Detroit was a bloodless coup. If you look at every situation overseas that the government goes in and takes out the leader and puts in their own public regime, it's the same thing that happened here in Detroit. They came in and destroyed the education, destroyed the real estate, took out the head person in charge and created chaos. And now they're restoring order the way they see fit by bringing in the emergency manager."

Report: relative calls Kwame Kilpatrick prosecution racist, Detroit brainwashed
mlive.com

Marion Barry, a former four-term black Democrat mayor of Washington, D.C., was affectionately nicknamed *"Mayor for Life."* He maintained this honorary title until his death, even though this "Chocolate City" was drug-infested and America's murder capital for consecutive years during most of his tenure. Furthermore, in 1990, the mayor was arrested and later convicted on drug charges after the FBI videotaped him smoking crack cocaine in a hotel. He served six months in a federal prison. And guess what was the alleged catalyst behind his arrest. No, it wasn't his notorious drug habit; it was racism. In his autobiography titled, *"Mayor For Life,"* Marion Barry explained:

"[t]hey didn't want me creating all of these opportunities for black folks. So when the FBI set me up at the Vista [Hotel], they were really trying to kill me. . . . The war to reclaim Washington for white people had been declared."

After his release from prison, he was elected to the Council of the District of Columbia in 1992, and then elected again as mayor in 1994, serving from 1995 to 1999. Overall, Barry served three tenures on the council of DC (1975-1979, 1993-1999, 2005 – until his death in 2014). Evidently, racism really held him down.

In 'Mayor for Life,' D.C.'s Marion Barry takes pride in himself but little blame for problems
washingtonpost.com

The race card isn't only played by big city Democrat mayors. The small, racially diverse town of Monticello, N.Y. — 29.3 percent black, 29.9 percent Hispanic, 34.6 percent white — had its black Democrat mayor slam it into play. It occurred after Mayor Gordon Jenkins drove to the scene of a serious car accident to survey the damage, and authorities noticed that he appeared to be intoxicated. They requested he take a Breathalyzer test. The mayor refused. As a result, he was arrested and taken to the police station. Upon arrival, the mayor shifted into full victim mode, and it was all captured on more than three hours of video. As reported by CBS:

In a video recorded at his own police headquarters, a man identified as Jenkins was shown seated in a chair with one hand handcuffed to a wall. During the first minute of the video, he is heard apparently talking to himself, using a variety of obscene insults to describe the officers.

Soon afterward, an officer comes in to interview him.

"You know something, Davis?" he says to the officer in the video. "I'm the one that hired you in this job, man. I mean, it doesn't matter. It doesn't matter about that. But you know something? How the f**k you guys going to play the game?"

When the officer later addresses him as "sir," Jenkins replies: "Don't call me sir."

"Mayor? Is that better?" the officer says.

"Don't call me mayor," Jenkins replies. "Call me n****r, because that's what I am when I'm right here in handcuffs. But you know something? I don't give a f**k."

Altogether, hours of video were released, showing Jenkins not happy about his arrest.

"What are you going to do? Put me in jail five years? I'll get out in five years, and I going to f***ing tell you what the f**k you did to me, and I'm going to come back to you," he tells an officer later.

The mayor was charged with DWI, refusing a Breathalyzer, obstruction of justice and criminal mischief.

The final charge came following an incident seen about an hour and 22 minutes into the first of three video clips. Jenkins stands up, pulls a clock off the wall, and hurls it out the door of the interrogation room while demanding to know who is at the police station desk.

"Why did you break the clock?" an officer says.

"Because I called you and you didn't answer, and you f***ed... these cuffs are too tight," Jenkins replies. When the officer returns to the room, Jenkins accuses the officer of trying to "humiliate" him.

Although the trustee of Monticello called for the mayor to step down following this incident, he maintained his position for almost two years before being removed by a New York state court. "Unscrupulous conduct" was cited as the court's reason for his forced resignation. Up until his removal, Gordon Jenkins was Monticello's mayor for seven years. He, along with his base, believes "something else" was the reason behind his forced exit. And of course, that "something else" is racism.

Video Shows Monticello Mayor Cursing, Breaking Clock After DWI Arrest
newyork.cbslocal.com

The IUPAC

What is the most abundant element in the universe? According to science, the answer is hydrogen. However, in the jaundiced eye of the RGI, the correct answer is racism. And I'm certain that the RGI wants racism added to the Periodic Table of Elements. Perhaps the International Union of Pure and Applied

Chemistry (IUPAC) should consider such a request. After all, the RGI has several studies that appear to validate racism being the most abundant element in the universe (well, black people's universe) and whites are harnessing its power.

Racism Causes Premature Births

All this time, I erroneously assumed that poor prenatal care and/or other factors contributed to premature births. Thankfully, this RGI endorsed study set things straight. As reported by *theroot.com:*

"A pair of Emory University studies released this year have connected the large share of African-American children born before term with the biologically detectable effects of stress created in women's bodies after decades of dealing with American racism. As shocking as that itself may sound, the studies' findings don't end there.

Racism, and its ability to increase the odds that a pregnant mother will deliver her child early, can kill. There is also evidence that racism can alter the capacity for a child to learn and distorts lives in ways that can reproduce inequality, poverty and long-term disadvantage, the studies found."

And for the cynics like me who doubt racism's impact, Elizabeth Corwin, Dean of Research at Emory University's Woodruff School of Nursing, wants you to know, *"Racism is an incredibly powerful force."* Doubling down on this assertion, Dr. Diane L. Rowley, a professor at the University of North Carolina at Chapel Hill's Gillings School of Global Public Health, stated:

"The research was at first just suggesting, but it's well-established today, something about living in the United States, something beyond poverty or health insurance coverage and health care access is helping to shape pregnancy outcomes," Rowley said. "And that something is racism."

According to the study, of the 15 million babies born prematurely each year in America, 16.8 percent are Black, 13.6 percent are Native American, 11.7 percent are Latino, 10.5 percent are White, and 10.3 percent are Asian.

Although most experts admit to not knowing all the reasons for early labor, racism has once again become the de facto answer; explicitly, the organic racism that Dr. Rowley believes is exclusively practiced by whites in America. Someone needs to inform the thousands of pregnant women who illegally cross the

U.S border (with pending anchor babies) that it's best to remain in their homeland. Why risk a premature birth because of America's inescapable racism when they can remain in their country and only worry about the Zika virus. Furthermore, since Asians lose the fewest babies, does that mean they're practicing reverse-racism on whites?

Racism Linked to Infant Mortality and Learning Disabilities
theroot.com

[Article's Quote: "A team of researchers closely tracked the pregnancies of more than 100 women during the last three months of their pregnancies."]

Racism Makes Black Men Age

Generally, people embrace flattering stereotypes of themselves or groups. One particularly favorable stereotype used in the black community is that "black don't crack." In other words, blacks age well. Just imagine how many black Benjamin Buttons would exist if racism didn't accelerate the rate that black men aged. Well, that's what researchers from the University of Maryland's medical school claim; racism detrimentally affects black men's aging process. As reported by the Daily Mail:

"Black men who are victims of racism literally age quicker than those who are not, a new study has found.

Their bodies speed up the biological process of ageing which means they are at risk of getting illnesses like diabetes or heart disease much younger than expected, it said.

It would explain why, in certain parts of the world, black people are more prone to some diseases than other races even allowing for age, income and other factors.

But the effects particularly apply to black people who have their own 'internalised bias' - in other words, they have negative views themselves about black people.

Those who are more 'pro black' are less likely to experience a speeding up of the ageing process, measured by DNA biomarkers of ageing on chromosomes in the body.

Researchers from the medical school of the University of Maryland conducted interviews and medical tests on 92 adult black men.

Their experiences included racism at the hands of police, prospective employers, public officials and everyday staff in stores or restaurants.

A psychological questionnaire also determined if the men themselves held any 'internal' bias against black people - in other words they had negative views without necessarily realising it."

Damn, once again, I was wrong. I erroneously attributed a tough aging process to lifestyle choices; e.g., diet, exercise, sleep, and genetics. Silly me, I need to start blaming racism more. It's a catch-all for black pathologies, and I have a few vices that I'd love to blame on racism. I'll probably have trouble convincing the wife, though. Ironically, the study concludes that pro-blacks are likely to live longer... in racist America.

Black men who experience racism age quicker than those who don't - and could stress be to blame?
dailymail.co.uk

Blacks Wait Longer to Cross Roads

Why did the chicken cross the road? I don't know, but if the following study has merit, the chicken definitely crossed the road faster than a black person did — unless, the black person was chasing the chicken.

"A new US study has found black people have to wait 32 percent longer at a crosswalk than white people before drivers chose to yield. Researchers at the University of Arizona also found that black pedestrians were twice as likely as white pedestrians to be passed by multiple vehicles. 'We were surprised at just how stark the difference was,' said transportation planning expert, Professor Arlie Adkins. The study involved 88 pedestrian trials and 173 drivers and was co-authored Portland State University researchers Kimberly Kahn and Tara Goddard. 'We are not saying drivers are overtly racist,' Kahn said, emphasising that the study results are consistent with implicit biases that individuals may hold beneath their awareness against certain groups of people."

Black people have to wait 32% LONGER than white people to cross the road: Study reveals extent of racism among drivers
dailymail.co.uk

Racism Makes Blacks Fat

Thanks to the following study, I finally understand why Oprah, even as a self-made billionaire, still possesses so many gripes with America. As reported by *Daily Mail*:

"There are many reasons why an increasing number of people are classified as obese - and now racism could be one of them. Frequent experiences of racism are associated with a higher risk of obesity among African American women, a new study claims. Scientists found that women who were more frequently victimised for their race, were more likely to be obese. The study, by Slone Epidemiology Centre at Boston University, found the relationship between racism and obesity was

strongest among women who reported consistently high experience of racism over a 12 year period. The research was based on the Black Women's Health Study, which enrolled 59,000 African-American women in 1995 and has followed them since. While rates of obesity in the U.S. have risen rapidly over the past few decades, the greatest increases have been seen in African American women, half of whom are currently classified as obese."

And for the blacks who have no weight issues, don't worry, I'm sure a grievance study is in the works for you somewhere. Racism can now be created out of thin air ensuring that no victim-minded person is left out.

Is racism making you FAT? Victims of prejudice are at greater risk of obesity
dailymail.co.uk

Mr. Sandman is Racist?

Who knew that Mr. Sandman — the folkloric, bringer of good dreams — was racist? Yes, a study has shown that he only brings the best dreams to white people. Dr. Lauren Hale, a family and preventative medicine professor at Stony Brook University, elaborated with *NPR.org* about a study from the Center for Disease Control (CDC).

"Race and ethnicity also tend to correlate with sleep. Nobody sleeps better than white people, according to the CDC report; 54 percent of non-Hispanic blacks get sufficient sleep, about 12 percent fewer than whites. "What is likely going on is probably explained by demographic composition," Hale says. "Densely populated neighborhoods might have more noise and light. African-Americans compared to whites are more likely to live in those neighborhoods."

On top of that, Hale says there are a lot of stressors that nonwhite communities disproportionately feel that can influence sleep. "There are concerns about racism, not being able to feed one's family, relatives being incarcerated," she says. "One needs to feel safe. If you don't have that internal feeling of security whether financial, physical or emotional, it will be harder to fall asleep."

Clearly, the study didn't include women in the "hood" whom I've categorized as "Quadruplers[7]" (Baby Mamas whose lifestyles are subsidized by taxpayers at least four different ways — housing, daycare, food stamps, medical, etc.); Quadruplers definitely get the best sleep.

Nobody Sleeps Better Than White People, Says Study
nymag.com

#OscarsSoWhite

The year is 1940, and the Twelfth Academy Awards is underway in Los Angeles. Hattie McDaniel has just won Best Supporting Actress for her role as Mammy in *Gone with the Wind.* She's the first black nominee/winner, and her acceptance speech was saturated with gratitude and humility:

"Academy of Motion Picture Arts and Science, fellow members of the motion picture industry and honored guests: This is one of the happiest moments of my life, and I want to thank each one of you who had a part in selecting me for one of the awards, for your kindness. It has made me feel very, very humble; and I shall always hold it as a beacon for anything that I may be able to do in the future. I sincerely hope I shall always be a credit to my race and to the motion picture industry. My heart is too full to tell you just how I feel, and may I say thank you and God bless you"

After her speech, she returned to a small table located in the ballroom's rear isolated from her fellow nominees. The seating arrangement wasn't her choice; it was mandated. Movie executives had to beg just to get her into the awards ceremony — held at a segregated "No Blacks" hotel. McDaniel was no stranger to discrimination. Jim Crow laws had also prevented her from attending the world premiere of *Gone with the Wind* in Atlanta. In spite of the racial barriers, she persevered. Equal opportunity to exhibit one's talent was the primary desire of black entertainers such as Hattie McDaniel.

Oscar's First Black Winner Accepted Her Honor in a Segregated 'No Blacks' Hotel in L.A.
hollywoodreporter.com

Now, fast-forward to the year 2016, where humble expectations of equal opportunity have evolved into hardcore demands for equal outcome. Several members of the RGI put on Oscar-worthy performances — of victimhood — after no blacks were nominated for Oscars in any major categories. The outrage sparked the hashtag #OscarsSoWhite. Al "Shakedown" Sharpton told Variety[8] magazine that his civil rights group would convene a series of meetings and conference calls with African-American leaders and advocacy groups to create a campaign encouraging people not to watch the awards show. Sharpton said in a statement[9]:

"Hollywood is like the Rocky Mountains, the higher up you get the whiter it gets. And this year's Academy Awards will be yet another Rocky Mountain

Oscars. Yet again, deserving black actors and directors were ignored by the Academy — which reinforces the fact that there are few if any blacks with real power in Hollywood."

Sharpton also criticized the industry for having a *"fraudulent image of progressive and liberal politics and policies."* His comments followed fellow card-carrying RGI member Spike Lee, who complained[10]:

"How Is It Possible For The 2nd Consecutive Year All 20 Contenders Under The Actor Category Are White? And Let's Not Even Get Into The Other Branches. 40 White Actors In 2 Years And No Flava At All. We Can't Act?! WTF!!."

Actress Jada Pinkett-Smith, whose husband Will Smith wasn't nominated for his leading role in "Concussion," stated that she wouldn't even watch the Oscars. She promoted the boycott through a lengthy Facebook video, saying in part[11]:

"Today is Martin Luther King's birthday, and I can't help but ask the question: Is it time that people of color recognize how much power, influence, that we have amassed, that we no longer need to ask to be invited anywhere?" Begging for acknowledgement, or even asking, diminishes dignity and diminishes power. And we are a dignified people, and we are powerful. So let's let the Academy do them, with all grace and love. And let's do us, differently."

The united front was really just a front to exploit white guilt. After all, taking advantage of white guilt has been an immensely beneficial strategy for the RGI. White guilt is the gift that keeps on giving. In fact, white guilt was utilized to provoke Academy members into voting for *"Twelve Years a Slave"* — an adaptation of the 1853 slave narrative memoir by Solomon Northup, a free black man who was kidnapped and sold into slavery. The Los Angeles Times noticed the guilt-tripping:

The film's distributor anchored its awards campaign around the line "It's time," easily interpreted as an attempt to exhort members of the Academy of Motion Picture Arts and Sciences into voting for the movie because it was the right thing to do.

The film's director, British filmmaker Steve McQueen, said repeatedly during the long awards season that Hollywood appeared more comfortable making Holocaust movies than slavery stories. And in her opening monologue, Oscar host Ellen DeGeneres even joked that if McQueen's telling of the enslavement of Solomon Northup didn't take the top Academy Award, voters could be branded as "racists."

Uh oh... calling whites the dreaded "r-word," and I don't mean "Republican" (although they're treated interchangeably today) is a proven game changer. Which is why two Oscar voters privately admitted that they voted for the movie without actually seeing it. The two claimed that they felt obligated to do so — given the film's social relevance. *Twelve Years a Slave* ultimately won three Academy Awards in 2014: Best Picture (black director), Best Supporting Actress for Lupita Nyong'o (black), and Best Adapted Screenplay for John Ridley (black). Noteworthy is the fact that that the president of the Academy of Motion Picture Arts and Sciences is black. The Academy has recently promised more diversity.

Two Oscar Voters Picked '12 Years A Slave' Without Watching It
huffingtonpost.com

"It's about opportunity to act, not awards," said actor Jamie Foxx, who in 2005 won a Best Actor Oscar for his role in Ray. I wholeheartedly agree with that notion. Additionally, instead of griping about the wrongs in Hollyweird, including the lack of black men playing leading roles, the RGI should focus on the lack of black men playing leading roles in black single-parent homes. Nevermind... that would break its covenant with the Democrat party; black single-parent homes are a vital voting bloc.

Despite the existence of countless black-specific award shows and film platforms — NAACP Image awards, BET (Black Entertainment Television) awards, American Black Film Festival, Pan-African Film Festival, San Francisco Black Film Festival, Hollywood Black Film Festival, Black Harvest International Film Festival, African Diaspora International Film Festival, New York African Film Festival, BlackStar Film Festival, etc. — the RGI still wants diversity to lean one way. Diversity is one of the seemingly agreeable buzzwords that the RGI effortlessly tosses around to find favor. But let's be clear, diversity essentially means "less white." They want white events diversified while black events remain black. In fact, the RGI desires every white-dominated platform to resemble the National Basketball Association's 2016 All-Star game, which featured only one white guy out of the selected twenty-six players. Actually, he was a "white Hispanic" and only got the All-Star nod as a replacement for an injured black guy. So, should the NBA All-Star game have more diversity for diversity's sake, or remain merit-based? I'll submit that question at the next NAACP awards show.

Heartless Racists

After complaining to his mother about sleeping difficulties and chest pains, fifteen-year-old Anthony Stokes was rushed to the hospital. The diagnosis was dire — dilated cardiomyopathy, an enlarged heart that's too weak to pump blood efficiently. A heart transplant was desperately needed; without one, doctors estimated he'd have less than a year to live. Stokes, who was wearing a court-ordered ankle monitoring bracelet during the diagnosis, later received even worse news; the hospital refused to place him on its heart transplant waiting list. Ultimately, this decision was a death sentence.

The teenager's family immediately suspected racism was the motive; however, the hospital cited Anthony's *"history of non-compliance"* in its letter to the family. The letter stated, *"Anthony is currently not a transplant candidate due to having a history of noncompliance, which is one of our center's contraindications to listing for heart transplant."* Dr. Ryan Davies, a cardiothoracic surgeon at the Alfred I. DuPont Hospital for Children — and not involved with this case — explained to CNN: *"Assessing compliance for potential transplant recipients is important because if a patient doesn't strictly take all required medicines as directed, he or she could die within weeks of leaving the hospital."* Dr. David Weill, medical director of Stanford University's Lung and Heart-Lung Transplant Program, also expressed to CNN that it's normal for patients to be rejected from organ transplant lists because of noncompliance — in other words, they are perceived as people who won't follow instructions about taking medications or keeping medical appointments. Arthur Caplan, head of the division of medical ethics at NYU Langone Medical Center, noted to CNN that patients have to adhere to a lifelong regimen after receiving an organ transplant — showing up at medical appointments, taking medications, monitoring changes in health — and teenagers, in general, don't have a good track record of following orders. Regardless, the family remained convinced that Anthony's denial wasn't due to his *"history of noncompliance."* A spokesperson for the family said a doctor told them that Anthony's low grades and time spent in juvenile detention factored into that assessment. *"It just seemed they decided he's a troublemaker, and that's not true[12],"* Anthony's mom told The Atlanta Journal-Constitution.

With accusations of stereotyping and racism, this story quickly moved onto the mainstream media's radar, and that's when the local RGI affiliate was ready to make its national debut. The president of Georgia's Southern Christian Leadership Conference chapter said Anthony was judged based on *"tattoos and an ankle bracelet"* from a *"juvenile agency,"* and was discriminated against *"because he was poor, black and had trouble with the law."* Those keywords put the collective black outrage into motion, and then media scrutiny mounted against the hospital. Within a week, the hospital — without explanation — reversed its decision; the teenager was placed on the list. Not only was he placed on the list, he was prioritized and moved to the front of the line. Although doctors initially informed Anthony that he'd likely receive a new heart in about three to four months (according to a family friend), surgery was successfully completed after just seven days from his placement on the list. A family friend attributed the story-book outcome to *"the handiwork of God and the media pressure."* Unsurprisingly, the true catalyst for the decision reversal didn't receive any credit... it never does. So, on the family's behalf, and from the kindness of my healthy heart, the race card is being publicly thanked.

Teen put on heart transplant list after earlier denial
cnn.com

'Noncompliance' bars 15-year-old Atlanta boy from heart transplant list
nydailynews.com

With a new heart and renewed lease on life, fifteen-year-old Anthony was set to create a future that contrasted his troubled past. *"So I can live a second chance. Get a second chance and do things I want to do[13],"* he told the local media. The heart transplant would help straighten out his life. Indeed, Anthony utilized the new heart and second chance at life to do the things he wanted to do. However, two years later, at the age of seventeen, Anthony was killed while doing the things he wanted to do. Unfortunately, those "things" included carjacking, home invasion, armed robbery and other felonious activities.

Apparently, old habits die hard, and those habits ensured that Anthony wouldn't get a third chance at life. As reported by *nydailynews.com*:

Stokes, of Decatur, allegedly carjacked a Honda, then burst into a Roswell home and shot at an elderly woman as he tried to rob her, WSB-TV reported. The woman was not hit.

"A lady said a person kicked in the door to break into the house. She was inside the living room and saw the suspect, who was wearing a mask," Lisa Holland, of the Roswell Police Department, told the news station.

Stokes then took off at a high speed as cops chased him down the highway. He smashed into a 33-year-old pedestrian before losing control and plowing into a pole.

"He did a fishtail spin going around to the right and hit a pedestrian. I saw a white shirt fly up in the air," witness Claudia Kuklis told WSB.

Police had to cut him from the mangled, carjacked vehicle

The seventeen-year-old later died at the hospital with a heart that was still practically under warranty. I can't confirm if the hospital issued an *"I told you so"* or *"Apology Accepted"* statement to the RGI and media. But, I am certain that the RGI attributes Anthony's cause of death to PTSD (Post Traumatic Slave Disorder) and not to career-criminal disorder.

Heart transplant recipient Anthony Stokes dies in police chase, crash
wsbtv.com

Troubled Ga. teen who received controversial heart transplant dead after crime spree ends in fatal wreck: cops
nydailynews.com

I know a guy who would've definitely put that heart to good use

Oprah's Cure for Racism

The RGI is heavily invested in agitprop because it needs blacks to believe that racism is metastasizing uncontrollably across America. Then, it'll promote RGI remedies. For example, Oprah Winfrey — the former undisputed queen of daytime talk, now undisputed queen of the RGI — has created her own remedy for racism.

Always the masterful marketer, she deliberately makes racially accusatory comments to boost promotion for her grievance movies. Once, she took issue with the manner that President Obama is criticized. During a BBC interview, she opined:

"There's a level of disrespect for the office that occurs. And that occurs in some cases and maybe even many cases because he's African-American. There's no question about that and it's the kind of thing nobody ever says but everybody's thinking it."

Oprah Winfrey: The Butler, racism and Obama
bbc.com

Interestingly, she failed to consider that President Obama enthusiastically campaigned (twice) to be subjected to the so-called *"level of disrespect"* that accompanies the office, and was twice successful. Moreover, she neglected to mention how America's stifling racism didn't prevent her from becoming a media mogul, or stop the trailblazing successes of other blacks such as Dr. Condi Rice, Robert "Bob" Johnson, Dr. Ben Carson, et al. Like Oprah, these individuals came from humble beginnings and stand as testaments to America's exceptionalism. Anyone notice that Oprah never defended Dr. Ben Carson or Dr. Condi

Rice whenever they were "disrespected" by racists — specifically black racists? I digress.

Oprah then proceeded to identify the ultimate source of the racism, and even candidly offered a cure — albeit an ominous cure:

"There are still generations of people, older people, who were born and bred and marinated in it, in that prejudice and racism, and they just have to die."

In other words, old whites are the problem. They're inherently racist, which in turn makes them incapable of judging people by the content of character. Thus, they must die!

Introducing OprahCare: the "Final Solution" for racism. Not only does OprahCare end racism, it silences Obama's critics — essentially, killing two racist birds with one righteous stone. Though, an obvious flaw with OprahCare is that it wants death for those who criticize Obama because of his race, yet, excuses those who won't criticize him because of his race. The OprahCare proponents refer to this contradiction as "payback." (Learn more about "payback" in the #BlackLivesMatter chapter.)

Unlike ObamaCare, where the public was assured that we could keep our doctor if we liked our doctor, OprahCare actually allows whites to keep their racist views if they like their racist views. The only stipulation is that they will *"have to die"* to keep them. Whites such as Donald Trump and Bill O'Reilly are immediate OprahCare enrollees who come to mind. I expect to see them on OprahCare brochures. On the other hand, white friends of the Grievance Diva such as Dr. Phil would receive waivers.

Although OprahCare may appear to target older white racists, its aim is broader. The other potential recipients of OprahCare are any white non-Democrats – definitely Republicans, Conservatives, Tea Partiers, and Libertarians. Even white Hispanics, such as George Zimmerman, are ideal for OprahCare. Granted, Zimmerman claimed to have voted for Obama (which is waiver-worthy), but he also killed Trayvon Martin, whom Oprah considered this generation's Emmett Till.

Oprah: Trayvon Martin The 'Same Thing' As Emmett Till (VIDEO)
huffingtonpost.com

Whites in other countries also qualify for OprahCare. For instance, the Swiss saleswoman who allegedly treated Oprah like a commoner when she (Oprah) inquired about a $38,000 Tom Ford handbag isn't exempt.

Oprah Winfrey's account of being racially profiled at Swiss boutique is 'not true,' shop clerk says
nydailynews.com

[Article's Quote: An unidentified Italian woman says, 'I don't know why someone as great as her would cannibalize me on TV' over a $38,000 Tom Ford handbag flap that has Switzerland in an uproar.]

White liberals are exempt from OprahCare as long as they continue to openly display white guilt. Naturally, blacks are exempt, despite a poll that concluded: *"[T]hirty-seven percent (37%) of American Adults think most black Americans are racist,"* while *"[j]ust 15% consider most white Americans racist, while 18% say the same of most Hispanic Americans."* Even so, OprahCare asserts that only whites can be racist, which apparently is acceptable if they're only being racist towards black conservatives. The RGI's conventional wisdom interprets broad generalizations of blacks as "racist," but justifies blacks' broad generalizations of others as "observations."

More Americans View Blacks As Racist Than Whites, Hispanics
rasmussenreports.com

Signing up for OprahCare isn't an option for whites; the Grievance Diva has already identified the racists, and their OprahCare policies have been pre-approved. They're simply waiting to be implemented.

OprahCare outreach coordinators wearing "So Sorry" shirts

Is Lowering the Bar Racist?

For at least a decade, blacks (excluding African immigrants) have maintained the anchor position regarding the achievement gap. The achievement gap is the observed, persistent disparity of educational measures between the performance of groups of students, especially groups defined by socioeconomic status, race/ethnicity, and gender. It can be detected on a variety of measures, including standardized test scores, grade point average, dropout rates, and college enrollment and completion rates. Federal and state educators continue to create policies and initiatives in an effort to tighten the widening achievement gap — even if those policies/initiatives sometimes cater to the lowest denominator or embrace low expectations.

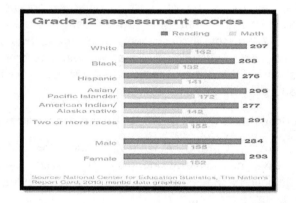

For example, in 2012, the state of Virginia proposed controversial education goals that lowered passing rates for blacks, Latinos, and students with disabilities but made the rates higher for white and Asian students. Patricia Wright, Virginia's superintendent of public instruction at the time, defended the policy:

"The concept here is that if indeed within six years we can close the achievement gap between the lowest- and highest-performing schools — at least cut it in half — that would be acceptable progress."

According to NPR, the updated passing rates were a result of Virginia's board of education analyzing students' test scores in reading and math. In math, the acceptable passing rate for Asian students was set at 82 percent, 68 percent for whites, 52 percent for Latinos, 45 percent for blacks, and 33 percent for kids with disabilities. Apparently, with educational goals for blacks near the level of students with disabilities, the old adage that black students have to *"work twice as hard"* doesn't apply here. The one upside of black students being placed at the bottom is that there's nowhere else to go but up. I guess this is the *"lead from behind"* strategy.

Firestorm Erupts Over Virginia's Education Goals
npr.org

Florida's board of education also wants to narrow the achievement gap by lowering of academic standards for black students. Florida only expects seventy-four percent of their black pupils to be proficient in Math and Reading (at grade level or better) by the year 2018. As far as Florida's expectations for its Asian/White/Latino students, seventy-four percent is an unacceptable indication of underachievement; such status is reserved for blacks. It expects 90 percent of Asian students, 88 percent of white students, and 81 percent of Hispanics students to be reading at or above grade level. For math, the goals are 92 percent of Asian kids to be proficient, whites at 86 percent, Hispanics at 80 percent and blacks at 74 percent.

Florida Passes Plan For Racially-Based Academic Goals
tampa.cbslocal.com

One frustrating aspect of this "cater to the lowest denominator" approach becomes apparent on graduation day. These schools don't issue the coddled, black graduates with diplomas that reflect their academic shortcuts. Instead, they receive the same diploma — once based on merit and successful comprehension of the core curriculum — as their diverse counterparts who were held to a higher standard. In other words, equal reward without equal effort.

In the STEM fields — Science, Technology, Engineering, Math — the dearth of black students is telling. It's a field where lowering the bar is ultimately detrimental to the individual. One typically has to possess the aptitude and work ethic to endure these challenging fields.

Despite the recent focus on improving and increasing STEM education in the United States, results from an online survey conducted by Harris Interactive on behalf of University of the Sciences show that over half (51 percent) of all high school-aged students are not interested in pursuing careers in healthcare and the sciences. Even more disconcerting is the increase in lack of interest from African American students, who are already tremendously underrepresented in the STEM workforce.

The 51 percent of 9th-12th grade students who say they are definitely or probably not considering a career in science or healthcare represents a 4.1 percent increase over last year's survey. The largest group contributing to this percentage is African Americans, with 61 percent of respondents declaring they are not interested in pursuing careers in healthcare and the sciences.

On the RGI's endless hunt for racism, it'll cite Silicon Valley and the overall tech industry's shortage of blacks as racism; even though the RGI knows that there's an urban perception that STEM is for THEM (Whites and Asians).

Minorities Represent Largest Sector Not Interested In Pursuing STEM Careers
prnewswire.com

Chapter II

#BlackLivesMatter

"Black lives do matter but it must matter to black people first."
— Arthur Reed (Ex-Gang Leader)

The RGI has many offspring, front organizations, and troll groups, but Black Lives Matter (BLM) is its militant wing and general purpose mob. This wholly-owned subsidiary of the RGI attempts to present itself as a simple grassroots movement spawned from injustice when in actuality, it's an AstroTurf movement spawned to create racial agitation/division, civil unrest, and lawlessness — while pushing a Marxist, anti-police agenda under the guise of "black issues." For the record, BLM's brand of Marxism is inspired by Karl Marx, not Groucho Marx; even though BLM's claimed impetus is hilarious like the latter. According to BLM's official website, the movement started[14]:

"[a]fter 17-year-old Trayvon Martin was post-humously [sic] placed on trial for his own murder and the killer, George Zimmerman, was not held accountable for the crime he committed."

For the last three and a half decades, blacks have accounted for more than half of America's homicide victims[15], yet a group that literally calls itself "Black Lives Matter" somehow didn't care to exist until Trayvon Martin was killed by George Zimmerman. Evidently, not even one of those black-on-black deaths prior to Zimmerman/Martin was sufficient to start a *"Black Lives Matter"* crusade. Furthermore, during the 503 days between Trayvon's death and Zimmerman verdict, thousands of blacks were murdered, but their killers didn't have George Zimmerman's pigmentation; they had George Jefferson's pigmentation. So, those lost lives — like the thousands that were killed pre, during, and post-Trayvon's life — didn't matter to a group that deliberately named itself "Black Lives Matter." Wikipedia states, *"Black Lives Matter (BLM) is an international activist movement, originating in the African American community that campaigns against violence toward black people."* Am I completely misunderstanding BLM, or simply realizing the real lies? Definitely, it's the latter!

"For every Trayvon Martin killed by someone not black, nine other blacks were murdered by someone black," wrote John W. Fountain, an award-winning journalist, and professor at Roosevelt University. He further elaborated about urban America's murder mania, which in 2015, spiked by 33 percent or more in Baltimore, St. Louis, and New Orleans:

"Imagine Soldier Field, home of the NFL's Chicago Bears, filled beyond capacity, brimming with 63,879 young African-American men, ages 18 to 24--more than U.S. losses in the entire Vietnam conflict. Imagine the University of Michigan's football stadium--the largest in the U.S.--filled to its limit of 109,901 with black men, age 25 and older. Now add 28,223 more--together totaling more than U.S. deaths in World War I. Picture two UIC Pavilions, home to the University of Illinois-Chicago Flames, packed with 12,658 Trayvon Martins--black boys, ages 14 to 17--nearly twice the number of U.S. lives lost in Iraq and Afghanistan. Now picture all of them dead. The national tally of black males 14 and older murdered in America over a 30-year period from 1976 through 2005, according to the Bureau of Justice Statistics: 214,661.The numbers tell only part of the story of this largely urban war, where the victims bare [sic] an uncanny resemblance to their killers."

As New York Justice Edward McLaughlin expressed to an urban terrorist during sentencing for attempted murder, *"Black lives don't matter to black people with guns[16]."* The deniers and apologists may lie about this reality but the numbers don't.

Our Dead Could Fill Our Stadiums
huffingtonpost.com

BLM's website reveals just as much about its non-actions as its actions. Firstly, judging from BLM's body of work, the term "Black Lives Matter" should have an asterisk. Clearly, only a specific kind of black life matters to the BLM movement. Secondly, the more accurate name or hashtag is *#BlackLivesMatterWhenTakenByWhites.* I'm guessing that this phrase is too long and more importantly, too honest for tee-shirts, so BLM settled for the first three words.

The Old vs. New

Although BLM is tethered to the RGI, it wants to become an independent movement with discernable differences between itself and the grievance vampires of old. At a rally in St. Louis for Michael Brown, a rapper/BLM activist declared, *"This ain't your* grandparents' civil rights movement," and veteran Civil Rights activist Barbara Reynolds agrees. "He's right," wrote Reynolds, an ordained minister, author, and former editor/columnist for USA Today. Her analysis continued:

"It looks, sounds and feels different. Black Lives Matter is a motley-looking group to this septuagenarian grandmother, an activist in the civil rights movement of the 1960s. Many in my crowd admire the cause and courage of these young activists but fundamentally disagree with their approach. Trained in the tradition of Martin Luther King Jr., we were nonviolent activists who won hearts by conveying respectability and changed laws by delivering a message of love and unity. BLM seems intent on rejecting our proven methods. This movement is ignoring what our history has taught.

The baby boomers who drove the success of the civil rights movement want to get behind Black Lives Matter, but the group's confrontational and divisive tactics make it difficult. In the 1960s, activists confronted white mobs and police with dignity and decorum, sometimes dressing in church clothes and kneeling in prayer during protests to make a clear distinction between who was evil and who was good.

But at protests today, it is difficult to distinguish legitimate activists from the mob actors who burn and loot. The demonstrations are peppered with hate speech, profanity, and guys with sagging pants that show their underwear. Even if the BLM activists aren't the ones participating in the boorish language and dress, neither are they condemning it.

I was a civil rights activist in the 1960s. But it's hard for me to get behind Black Lives Matter.
washingtonpost.com

Yusra Khogali, Toronto Black Lives Matter co-founder, used Facebook to set the record straight regarding the change of guard. She also updated whites on how they'll be impacted by the policy changes: *"What wypipo (white people) don't understand is that this is not like our elders movement. We will snatch ur edges and clap back you into ashes. We will also beat that ass becky. Run up."* Using coded speech to threaten others gives BLM plausible deniability when convenient.

Yusra K. Ali
March 30 at 1:44pm ·

What wypipo don't understand is that this is not like our elders movement. We will snatch ur edges and clap back you into ashes. We will also beat that ass becky. Run up.

Share

97

Indisputably, a generational divide has manifested between veterans and rookies. Whether it's Jesse Jackson being booed[17] in Ferguson, Rep. John Lewis saying that Black Lives Matter protesters should respect everyone's right to be heard[18], or Rep. Elijah Cummings being called derogatory names during the Baltimore riots, the quarrel has gone public.

> **Jon Swaine** ✓
> @jonswaine
>
> Loudspeaker: "This is congressman Elijah Cummings." Several men, loud and in unison: "Fuck you, n---."
> Cummings: "I'm begging you. Go home"
>
> 7:10 PM - 28 Apr 2015
>
> **213** RETWEETS   **78** LIKES

> **Matt Zapotosky** ✓
> @mattzap
>
> Congressman Elijah Cummings addresses crowd. Some yell profanity in response, throw middle fingers.
>
> 7:11 PM - 28 Apr 2015 from Baltimore, MD
>
> **74** RETWEETS   **33** LIKES

At a rally organized by Al Sharpton's NAN in Washington D.C., BLM activists stormed the stage[19] — after NAN officials reportedly denied them access — and claimed that the old regime was attempting to hijack the Black Lives Matter movement. Ashley Yates, co-founder of BLM affiliate group *Millennial Activists United*, took to Twitter to *"air dirty laundry"* about Sharpton who praised the young leaders' work at a summit convened by the White House, but never joined their protests or attended any action planning sessions. Moreover, Yates claims that Sharpton had *"not a single word[20]"* to say to the young activists when the meeting was over. The consensus of the new generation is that Sharpton wants to claim these splinter groups without showing any substantive interest in the work they've been doing. Pastor Danny Givens Jr., the clergy liaison to Black Lives Matter in Minneapolis, stated that they (old guard) *"want to co-opt the [Black Lives Matter] movement by presenting an olive branch and unity in order to promote their own agenda. These are preachers who have been doing this for 30 years or more and they don't want to make room for the next generation of faith leaders."*

Black clergy group apologizes for "intolerance" by some black pastors
startribune.com

During a NAN meeting, Shakedown Sharpton forcefully responded to the youngsters' sentiment and tried to convince them that they're being manipulated by others: *"It's the disconnect that is the strategy to break the movement. And they play on your ego. 'Oh, you young and hip, you're full of fire. You're the new face.' All the stuff that they know will titillate your ears. That's what a pimp says to a ho."* Sharpton essentially wants to control BLM's trajectory/development and complete the training of the fledgling activists. Only then, will they be able to fully join the dark side.

Amid tensions, Sharpton lashes out at younger activists
capitalnewyork.com

The Christian Science Monitor highlighted BLM's rebuke of a top-down leadership:

"In years past, the civil rights mantle of Martin Luther King Jr. was taken up by other charismatic leaders, political figureheads such as Jesse Jackson and Al Sharpton – each a skilled orator with roots in the black church, which in many ways is still the center of community life and politics for black Americans.

But as the country remembers Dr. King on Monday, a new generation of activists is doing things differently. Many within the Black Lives Matter movement are uncomfortable with venerating any "great man" of the past, and they reject the idea that any dynamic figurehead should embody their struggle today.

Younger protesters are doing much of their work through social media, and they're deciding that the social conservatism of many black churches is part of mistakes of the past. Many of these activists also say that the Black Lives Matter Movement owes a greater debt to the organizing principles of Occupy Wall Street than to the civil rights movement."

Although BLM is comprised of individuals growing up in a vastly different America than their predecessors — i.e. Mississippi isn't still burning, Jim Crow is dead, there's a black First Family etc. — the grievances inexplicably remain the same.

For Black Lives Matter, MLK's kind of activism isn't the only way
csmonitor.com

Oprah Winfrey, critical of BLM's lack of leadership, voiced her concerns during an interview promoting "Selma" — the film she produced about the 1965 protests in Alabama over voting rights for blacks. The queen of the RGI told People magazine:

"I think it's wonderful to march and to protest and it's wonderful to see all across the country, people doing it," she says. "But what I'm looking for is some kind of leadership to come out of this to say, 'This is what we want. This is what we want. This is what has to change, and these are the steps that we need to take to make these changes, and this is what we're willing to do to get it.'"

The response from BLM supporters was swift. The verdict was in; Oprah was guilty of being an out of touch elitist. The judgment made her clutch her pearls.

Protesters slam Oprah over comments that they lack 'leadership'
washingtonpost.com

Black Lives Matter is demanding to be the face of the victimization narrative this century. They are not waiting for the torch to be passed. However, understand that the differences between the old schoolers and new schoolers are tactical, not philosophical.

Obama Brings Black Lives Matter and Civil Rights Activists Together for Meeting
time.com

BLM's Strategy

If the only tool one has is a hammer, everything tends to be treated as nails. That's BLM's conflict resolution approach. BLM merges some traditional Civil Rights era strategies with social media blasts to its tactic of direct confrontation. And voila, a toxic brew of grievances via coordinated chaos is then poured onto society. Phillip Agnew, co-founder of the BLM affiliate group *Dream Defenders*, told reporters:

"We and people around the country are going to continue to take to the streets, we're going to continue to disrupt the daily order and ensure that business doesn't happen as usual until something happens for the people in our communities and we see some meaningful reform and clear indications from not only the president's office, but from governors, mayors, and police chiefs and officers around this country, that Black lives do truly matter."

This Ain't Your Granddaddy's Civil Rights Movement
bet.com

BLM is powered by negative energy placed into motion. In other words, it's sustained by an emotion (energy + motion) that's negatively charged. This emotional (instead of logical) approach can easily be seen and verified through its protest methodologies. It is unconcerned with the fact that these antagonizing ploys for immediate gratification have caused long-term, irreparable damage to its reputation. Admittedly, BLM does an excellent job of disruption; but just as atheists are quicker to burn a Bible than a Koran, BLM knows its limits. BLMers will hit soft targets or low-hanging fruit; places that have no influence or even played a part in the "oppression." Interestingly, BLMers never attempt to disrupt the flow of anything in the black community that would potentially stop black-on-black homicides. Overall, the protests are attention-whoring endeavors. And when an actual tragedy occurs that takes some shine away from BLM — such as the Paris attacks — BLM supporters will huff and puff as if victimization is BLM-exclusive. How dare other people besides BLM receive attention for their suffering! The audacity! The nerve!

Demonstrations

Apparently, stores, malls, city streets, and highways across America are oppressing blacks and thus need to be confronted. BLM has disrupted activity at many innocuous places — unworried that the commotion may ultimately hurt the very people it claims to serve — while triumphantly detailing their activity on social media with incident-specific hashtags. Cutting off its nose to spite its face is a standard RGI ploy. Comedian/activist Dick Gregory once called for a boycott[21] of Florida's tourism and agricultural industries (specifically Disney and orange producers) to help eliminate the Stand Your Ground Laws, while racial grievance guru Jesse Jackson told CNN[22], *"No doubt, the inclination is to boycott Florida, stop conventions, to isolate Florida as a kind of apartheid state."*

Black Lives Matter protest shuts down Mall of America and airport terminal
theguardiancom

[Author's Note: America's largest shopping mall was locked down after hundreds of protesters gathered for a Black Lives Matter demonstration that also caused an airport terminal to shut down.]

#BlackJobsDontMatter during the busy season

One cold winter day in January 2015, a group of BLM demonstrators hopped out of a rented van on Interstate 93 in Massachusetts, unrolled barrels — each filled with 1,200 pounds of concrete — and chained themselves to the barrels. Thousands of commuters were inconvenienced, particularly, an ambulance carrying an 83-year-old man who was seriously injured when his pickup truck skidded on ice and smashed into a stand of trees. Due to the BLM-induced congestion, the ambulance had to be diverted from a nearby hospital in Boston to one in Brocton, delaying this senior from receiving necessary hospital care in the process. State Police and firefighters had to saw the barrels and tubing loose to clear the highway. Twelve protesters were arrested, and at their sentencing, heard an impact statement from the 83-year-old man's daughter. Also, the judge called the protesters' actions "foolish," and added, *"One man in an ambulance had a beautiful life that mattered."* The protesters never explained how shutting down a major highway helped their cause. Oh, it didn't.

BLACK LIVES MATTER PROTEST HALTS TRAFFIC ON 405 FREEWAY
abc7.com

Judge scolds Black Lives Matter protesters, who get probation
enterprisenews.com

Political Rallies

When was the last time BLM crashed a corner of drug dealers? Oh, I remember... It happened somewhere around the time when the cow jumped over the moon. Instead of confronting the urban corner-clusters, crashing political campaign rallies (using intimidation tactics) is prioritized — even if the candidates such as Sen. Bernie Sanders and Hillary Clinton play for BLM's team. Assumingly, Sen. Sanders, a socialist's socialist who wants to give away more "free" stuff than other Democrat politicians do, and calls for an end to over-policing in black neighborhoods and systemic racism[23], is adored by BLM. Within a month's span, the group made its presence felt at two of his speaking engagements. MSNBC reported on the second encounter that occurred in the liberal utopia of Seattle, Washington:

"We're shutting this event down — now," said an activist who suddenly leapt on stage. She approached the microphone where Sanders had just begun speaking, thanking attendees for welcoming him to "one of most progressive cities in the United States of America." An event organizer attempted to stop the activist, and a heated exchange ensued as the crowd booed.

Eventually, activist Marissa Johnson was allowed to speak. "I was going to tell Bernie how racist this city is, even with all of these progressives, but you've already done that for me. Thank you," she said as some in the crowd called for her arrest.

Johnson then asked for a four-and-half-minute moment of silence to honor Michael Brown Jr., the black teenager who was killed by police in Ferguson, Missouri, a year ago. As the crowd grew more agitated, Johnson added that Sanders says he cares about grassroots movements, but, "The biggest grassroots movement in this country right now is Black Lives Matter."

Sanders stood by silently the entire time. Eventually, organizers decided to end the event and the Vermont senator did not return to the microphone.

Although Sen. Bernie Sanders was an active participant in the 60's Civil Rights movement, and his record on fighting for Civil Rights is longer than the weaves worn by BLM's professional disrupters, none of it mattered to their short-sighted, estrogen-driven agenda.

Bernie Sanders event shut down by Black Lives Matter activists
msnbc.com

Senator Bernie Sanders felt "the Bern" after his threesome with BLM

Hillary Clinton, the wife of former president Bill Clinton, who was affectionately called America's *"first black president"* by *blacks,* hosted a private, five-hundred dollar per plate event. Black Lives Matter activists crashed[24] her Grey Poupon-laden soirée demanding that she account for some of her past statements on racial justice. BLM claims that as First Lady, she supported her husband's 1994 crime bill, which led to an increase in mass incarceration, three-strike federal sentencing laws, the elimination of rehabilitative programs for drug abuse, and emphasized prison_construction. All of which disproportionately affected blacks. Hillary should've reminded BLM that she's married to an honorary black man, and thus exempt from black criticism. Alternatively, her campaign stated that different policies make sense at different times; therefore, today's Hillary Clinton is calling for *"facing up to the reality of systemic racism"* and ending the school-to-prison pipeline. In other words, she's speaking from both sides of her mouth.

Sign quotes Clinton's 1996 statement regarding at-risk youth: *"We have to bring them to heel."*

When BLM protesters appeared at a Hillary campaign event in Philadelphia PA., Bill Clinton vehemently defended his 1994 crime bill and even had harsh words for the heckling BLMers. In grievance-speak, America's first (unofficial) black president was suddenly "acting white." Nation Public Radio (NPR) reported:

He said the bill lowered the country's crime rate, which benefited African-Americans, achieved bipartisan support, and diversified the police force. He then addressed a protester's sign, saying:

"I don't know how you would characterize the gang leaders who got 13-year-old kids hopped up on crack and sent them out onto the street to murder other African-American children," Clinton said, addressing a protester who appeared to interrupt him repeatedly. "Maybe you thought they were good citizens .... You are defending the people who kill the lives you say matter. Tell the truth. You are defending the people who cause young people to go out and take guns."

Noticeably, the lynch mob didn't (and won't) hold the Congressional Black Caucus (CBC) accountable for endorsing the 1994 crime bill. The feigned rage is simply another "blame whitey" scenario for black people's problems, and then guilt-trip whites into fixing those problems. Even though Clinton Inc. and other limousine liberals are amongst a dwindling group that still tolerates BLM's temper-tantrums, tolerance from typical white liberals in the real world has to be waning. It's obvious that BLM wants friends but doesn't want to be a friend.

Bill Clinton Gets Into Heated Exchange With Black Lives Matter Protester
npr.org

[Author's Note: Bill Clinton violated a major tenet of the Democrat Party; never speak about black apathy and hypocrisy regarding pervasive black criminality... Only reinforce positive black imagery! Additionally, embrace and "appreciate" any verbal abuse from blacks, regardless of its hostility level. After all, blacks are going to vote for the party anyway, so grin and bear it.]

Black Caucus yields on crime bill
articles.baltimoresun.com

Die-Ins

A die-in, sometimes known as a lie-in, is a form of protest where participants simulate being dead. In the simplest form of a die-in, protesters simply lie down on the ground and pretend to be dead; sometimes even covering themselves with signs or banners. The insincerity of BLM die-ins is that its die-ins never occur in places where blacks are literally dying, such as the hood. BLM's die-ins are simply grandstanding gestures in front of non-threatening whites.

BLM die-in at the finish line of the 2015 Twin Cities Marathon with a sign that read, *"Fuck Yo Finish Time"*

#BlackBrunch

Under the hashtag #BlackBrunch, BLMers invaded restaurants, diners, or eateries frequented by whites in affluent or gentrified neighborhoods. The best diners to disrupt were the hipster diners. Apparently, they're hotbeds of police brutality. While white hipsters enjoyed their overpriced omelets or Pabst beers, BLMers would read the names of black people killed by cops — and they didn't use their "inside voices" while reading. Instead, they yelled and behaved as if they possessed the absolute moral authority to castigate the patrons for eating while white. Although visibly bewildered, the customers would usually pause until the storm passed. Yet, another protest in a place that has nothing to do with the reason for the protest.

#BrunchingWhileWhite < #BlackBrunch

Vendetta = Violence

The RGI knows that resentment against whites is a core emotion within many blacks. And as Jedi Master Yoda sagely identified, *"Anger leads to hate... Hate leads to suffering."* Indeed, the underlying antipathy has led to suffering (from the victim mindset) and violence against whites. And yes, I've actually used a Yoda quote.

Dr. Thomas Sowell, the intellectual juggernaut, noticed the pattern of attacks and concluded that a black and white race war is in effect. He wrote[25]:

"Initial skirmishes in that race war have already begun, and have in fact been going on for some years. But public officials pretend that it is not happening, and the mainstream media seldom publish it at all, except in ways that conceal what is really taking place."

Former Congressman Allen West echoed Dr. Sowell's sentiment and added[26]:

"We were supposed to be living in a post-racial America since we elected the first 'African-American' president. That's hardly the case."

I have a tremendous amount of respect and admiration for these men. They're not RGI members or stockholders of victimology. Contrarily, these black men are straight-shooting realists who emphasize critical thinking over critical complaining. Moreover, they want to do what's right for America instead of what's best for a few Americans. However, despite my admiration, I disagree with their assessment that the continued black-on-white violence indicates a present or future race war. A race war requires at least two engaging races: the reoccurring black/white interracial violence is statistically overwhelmingly one-sided. More whites are killed annually by blacks than vice versa.

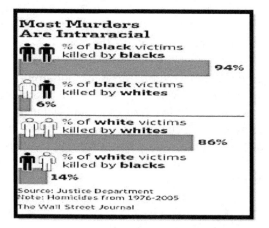

Hate Facts

Still, I maintain that it's not a race war. These assaults are simply considered payback. And this "payback" has been happening for decades with the RGI's blessings *(White victim + Black culprit = Payback/racial revenge)*. Since whites are generally perceived by many blacks as universal oppressors who consistently use institutionalized racism as a weapon of mass (black) destruction, black-on-white offenses are typically regarded as justified payback for white persecution. Actor Jamie Foxx exemplified this mindset while promoting his movie (Django). He joyously proclaimed[27]:

"I kill all the white people in the movie. How great is that? And how black is that?"

Imagine a white actor saying, *"I get to whip black people in the movie. How great is that? And how white is that?"*

Even the white liberals who proudly display their *"Hope & Change"* bumper stickers and *"Black Lives Matter"* sympathies can't escape the perception that whites are inherently racist. In fact, white liberals are simply viewed as whites who internalize their racism, whereas white conservatives are considered shamelessly racist. The former may actually be despised more than the latter. Either way, the victim mentality emphasizes that "good and bad" whites are simply opposite sides of the same racist coin. George Yancy, a black professor of philosophy at Emory University, blatantly stated in his New York Times article, *"Dear White America[28]"* that *"Being a 'good' white person or a liberal white person won't get you off the hook."*

Black-on-white violence rarely receives condemnation from the black press, and unsurprisingly, the mainstream media also conveniently overlook this pattern of racial violence; it conflicts with the portrayal of blacks as permanent victims incapable of being racists. Therefore, the non-coverage is just another instance of the corporate media spitting at the public and reporting it as rain.

Undoubtedly, white resistance is surfacing, and I believe this observation sparked Dr. Sowell's commentary. Nevertheless, the mounting white backlash is more of an awareness campaign and shedding of "white guilt," than one of violence.

Dr. Sowell also mentioned that he was appreciative that old age may spare him from seeing a race war. I say, enjoy the remainder of your earthly time because there is not, and will not be a race war. Laughably, the New Black Panthers have been endlessly calling for a race war, but the New Black Panthers are as relevant on racial matters as the Carolina Panthers (NFL football team). Nonetheless, "payback" attacks will continue with BLM's tacit encouragement. And sometimes, only divine intervention can postpone those attacks from occurring. Such was the case when Toronto Black Lives Matter co-founder Yusra Khogali used Twitter to beg *"Allah"* to stop her from killing *"white folks."* She tweeted, *"Plz Allah give me strength to not cuss/kill these men and white folks out here today. Plz plz plz."*

Yusra
@YusraKhogali

Plz Allah give me strength to not cuss/kill these men and white folks out here today. Plz plz plz.

2016-02-09, 10:57 AM from Toronto, Ontario

Moving to Saudi Arabia would solve her problem

"Payback" Instances

Most people know the name of that white Hispanic guy who stood his ground in Sanford, Florida, but certainly, many don't know the name of the white Hispanic who didn't stand his ground in Washington, D.C. His name is Chris Marquez, a decorated Iraq war veteran whose bravery inspired two statues. He was brutally attacked and robbed by a pack of black feral teens after they approached him and asked whether "black lives matter." The decorated Marine was eating in a McDonald's when the miscreants surrounded him and began yelling, *"Black lives matter."* At that point, they demanded he answered the question, *"Do you believe black lives matter?"* He didn't respond. *"I felt threatened and thought they were trying to intimidate me, so I figured I'm just going to keep to my food, eat my food and hopefully they'll leave me alone,"* Marquez told WJLA. The youths then started calling him a racist, he said. When he proceeded to leave the restaurant, the name-calling spiraled into a physical assault. One of the teens hit him in the head from behind, knocking Marquez unconscious to the ground, where the gang beat and robbed him. Marquez told police that one youth hit him in the head with what he believed was a handgun, which couldn't have been the case because D.C. has a gun ban. Surely, this criminal wouldn't dare violate the gun ban.

The veteran, who had survived ambushes in Fallujah, awoke on McDonald's sidewalk with his pants ripped and his wallet — containing $400 in cash, three credit cards, and his Veterans Affairs medical card, among other things — stolen. Washington D.C. police said they weren't considering the incident a hate crime. It takes no imagination to envision the black ethnic response had the marine shot and killed the domestic assailants as he once did foreign assailants.

Former Marine, AU student says he was beaten in racially motivated attack

washingtonpost.com

VETERAN ROBBED & BEATEN AT MCDONALD'S

During his time in the Corps, Marquez deployed to Iraq three times and Afghanistan once. He served eight years on active duty in the Marines as a rifleman and scout sniper from 2003-2011 and was awarded a Bronze Star for valor on his first deployment for carrying his commander's body out of combat after he died in an ambush. Marquez is the subject of the "No Man Left Behind" statues, at Camp Lejuene and Camp Pendleton, depicting him and another man holding up a wounded soldier at the Battle of Fallujah.

Two white teens, Jourdan Bobbish and Jacob Kula, were murdered execution-style in a Detroit field, and their lifeless bodies were discovered days later. They were robbed, tortured, and then murdered after trying to buy drugs. Their black killers, Fredrick Young and Felando Hunter, were sentenced to life in prison. During sentencing, the victims' families read impact statements. Jacob Kula's mother lamented, *"Not only did the defendant take away my son's future; he took away my future – my future as a mother – my future as a grandmother,"* Jourdan Bobbish's mother grieved, *"I have sorrow in my heart, soul and every fiber of my being today and I will carry that with me for the rest of my life."*

After hearing their touching statements, defendant Fredrick Young had something to say to the court. He wanted to apologize... BLM-style:

"I'd like to say sorry to the families of Aiyanna Jones, Michael Brown, Eric Garner. I want to apologize to them for not being able to get justice for their loved ones who was murdered in cold blood – and in respect for the peaceful protest, I want to say hands up don't shoot. Black lives matter – that's it your honor."

With no apology to his dead victims or their eternally impacted families, I was hoping that he'd at least apologize for being born.

Yellow is an appropriate jumpsuit color for this coward who gave a BLM-inspired speech

BLM Investors

Rapper Jay-Z and his wife Beyoncé are huge supporters of the Black Lives Matter movement. In fact, Mic.com reported that Jay-Z's global music and entertainment platform Tidal, in association with Roc Nation planned to donate $1.5 million to Black Lives Matter and several other local and national social justice organizations. The majority of recipients are social justice groups and organizations specifically committed to ensuring the nation understands that black lives matter. Tidal strategically made the announcement about its donation on what would've been Trayvon Martin's twenty-first birthday. The money was raised from a sold-out charity concert held in Brooklyn, New York, which featured

Beyoncé, Nicki Minaj, Jay-Z, Lil Wayne, and Nick Jonas. Jay-Z and Beyoncé's philanthropic endeavor shouldn't be surprising. During the Ferguson Fiasco of 2014 and Baltimore Tsunami of 2015, Hip Hop's First Family secretly bankrolled tens of thousands of dollars in bail money to protesters. Dream Hampton, Jay-Z's ghostwriter for his book *"Decoded,"* publicized the power couple's covert financial support in a sequence of tweets — before quickly deleting them. She doubled-down on her statements in an email sent to the New York Daily News: *"I can say I've personally helped facilitate donations they've given to protesters directly and that they never ask for anything in return, especially publicity."* Hmmm... I wonder why they don't contribute to the witness relocation program to combat the no-snitch mentality.

Jay Z's Tidal to Donate $1.5 Million To Black Lives Matter, Other Social Justice Groups
mic.com

Jay Z, Beyoncé donated bail for Baltimore, Ferguson protesters: writer
nydailynews.com

The money contributed by Hip Hop's Barack and Michele Obama is mere pennies on the dollar when compared to the money disbursed by the chief financier of BLM's instigated methods of social justice — left-wing billionaire George Soros. In an online poll conducted by Human Events, George Soros was voted, *"the single most destructive leftist demagogue in the country."* In 1998, Soros wrote, *"Insofar as there are collective interests that transcend state boundaries, the sovereignty of states must be subordinated to international law and international institutions."* According to Soros's private foundation tax filings — uncovered by the Washington Times — Soros donated $33 million dollars to dozens of different social justice organizations, to help turn events in Ferguson (Missouri), from a local protest into a national flashpoint. The billionaire's funding financed the bussing of professional organizers from Washington, D.C., and New York into Missouri. The numerous organizations reportedly created their own online 'echo chamber', by using their extensive social media presences to synchronize 'likes', reposts and comments on articles reflecting their point of view. BLM is just one of his pawns to push other agendas to divide America. It is cannon fodder for a broader battle. Soros knows that a house divided against itself cannot stand.

George Soros funds Ferguson protests, hopes to spur civil action
washingtontimes.com

The Overseer

#CutTheCheck

Famed BLMer, DeRay McKesson[29], quit his school administrator job in Minnesota to become a professional protester for the RGI. So, what happens when the RGI's money doesn't trickle down to its hired agitators in a timely fashion? Naturally, the employees will become restless and bite the hand that's supposed to feed them. When Ferguson became ground zero for racial frenzy, the RGI's rent-a-mob tactic caused dissention after the hired protesters didn't receive their pay. Suddenly, the only black lives that mattered to the professional protesters were their black livelihoods (#BlackLivelihoodsMatter). As a result, they created a #CutTheCheck hashtag and even held a sit-in at the offices of *MORE* (Missourians Organizing for Reform and Empowerment). *MORE* is the updated Missouri branch of *ACORN* (Association of Community Organizations for Reform Now), which filed for bankruptcy in late 2010. Investigative journalist and author Matthew Vadum[30] uncovered that *MORE* has been active in the Ferguson protests and in efforts to free jailed demonstrators so they can continue vandalizing businesses, intimidating perceived adversaries, setting fires, and throwing projectiles and human waste at cops.

MillenialAU (MAU), one of the BLM umbrella groups that participated in a sit-in, wrote an open, grievance letter to the white overseers of BLM-related finances, and posted it online.

"On May 14, 2015 many individuals and organizations of the protest movement that began in Ferguson, Missouri organized a sit-in in the office of Missourians Organizing for Reform and Empowerment (MORE). The demand was simple: Cut the checks.

Early in the movement, non-profit organization MORE, formerly known as the St. Louis chapter of ACORN, and local St. Louis organization Organization for Black Struggle created a joint account in which national donors from all over the world have donated over $150,000 to sustain the movement. Since then, the poor black [sic] of this movement who served as cash generators to bring money into St. Louis have seen little to none of that money. Furthermore, since the influx of funding has started, poor black people continue to take to the streets all the while losing their homes, vehicles, ability to feed themselves and their families, and suffering from trauma and mental illness with no ability to afford quality mental health services. Questions have been raised as to how the movement is to sustain when white non-profits are hoarding monies collected of off [sic] black bodies? When we will [sic] hold the industry of black suffering accountable? The people of the community are fed up and the accountability begins here and now.

This isn't about MORE. This is about black lives in the Black Lives Matter movement who are literally broke and starving. There is an insidious strand of racism and white supremacy that exists in this movement and it is called the Non-Profit Industrial Complex. As a by-product, it provides decent salaries and comfort to many people who are not affected by the disparities that they are trying to address. This money is typically in the hands of white people who oversee the types of services that the non-profit provides, while having select token black people to spearhead the conversations within and to the community.

We NEED to be thinking about justice for black people. This means white people must renounce their loyalty to the social normalcy that maintains white power and control. If black lives really matter, justice and self-determination for black people would mean the black community would control it's [sic] own political and economic resources.

It is asinine to believe that black people can continue to organize and take to the street when they can barely meet their basic needs. In St. Louis, organizers and protesters depleted $50,000 of the available funds and dispersed it among the people in the movement in no particular order. Jeff Ordower, executive director of MORE, stated that another $57,000 is expected in the next one to two weeks in which those funds will also be dispersed to the black people in the movement.

Moving forward, we are building a board of accountability within this movement. We must funnel economic into this movement through the hands of black people who are fighting with and for black life. More on this board will be discussed as we develop."

Remember, BLM isn't fighting for equality; it's fighting to generate and maintain salaries. #BlackLivelihoodsMatter

Hired Black Lives Matter protesters start #CutTheCheck after being stiffed by ACORN successor group
washingtontimes.com

Library Bans BLM

Majority-black Nashville, Tennessee is ranked number forty-five on *NeighborhoodScout.com's* list of "Most Dangerous Cities – 2016." One's chances of becoming a victim of either violent or property crime there are one in 20. Relative to Tennessee, Nashville's crime rate is 87 percent higher than the other cities and communities. So, who did Nashville's chapter of Black Lives Matter place into its crosshairs? Of course, it wasn't Nashville's black thugs — that move would violate its Hypocritical Oath *(Refer to Hypocritical, not Hippocratic Oath Chapter)*. Nashville's Public Library was targeted.

Black Lives Matter conducted its chapter meetings at the North Branch Library in North Nashville until library officials informed BLMers that events excluding groups of people could not be held inside the city's libraries. BLM accused the library of practicing *"white supremacy,"* but the truth (as truth usually is) was simple; so simple that BLM made it complicated. As a taxpayer-funded entity, Nashville's library system — which has an entire department devoted to Civil Rights — has a policy that mandates all meetings at their facilities be open to the public and news media. It has an open-door, open-meeting policy. It wasn't until a complaint from a library patron, who saw a BLM advertisement about an upcoming meeting and felt excluded, alerted the library staff to Black Lives Matter's exclusionary policy. The library was previously unaware of the group's racist rule, which allows blacks as well as non-blacks of color to attend but prohibits whites.

Naturally, the library's decision outraged Black Lives Matter, who then responded with its standard blame-game talking point. *"Due to white supremacy in our local government, this week's BLM General Body Meeting location has changed,"* BLM posted on its Facebook page. *"We were surprised about it, but we shouldn't have been,"* a BLM member told The Tennessean of the library's decision. *"We kind of know the history about how this goes in this country. ... It's definitely something we want to make public to tell people what's going on in the city."*

The group moved its meetings to a church where I assume it's acceptable to yell racism while practicing racism. I only pray that a wise soul in that church humbly asks, "What would Jesus do?"

Black Lives Matter 'color-only' rule runs afoul of Nashville library
tennessean.com

Black Lives Matter Nashville
February 19 at 8:49am ·

*****This is a disclaimer that the comments posted under this thread may be triggering for some audiences. Please proceed to read them at your own discretion*****

BLM General Body Meeting location has changed. See you tomorrow!

Due to white supremacy in our local government, this week's BLM General Body Meeting location has changed.
We will meet at Dixon Memorial United Methodist Church (1111 Buchanan Street Nashville, TN 37208) at 10am!

BLM General Body Meetings are open to black and non-black people of color only

BLM doesn't understand simple math... Racism + Racism = Racism

Chapter III

Hypocritical, not Hippocratic Oath

"Every veil secretly desires to be lifted, except the veil of hypocrisy."
– Richard Garnett

A Hippocratic Oath holds those who swear to it to a strict code of professional and personal conduct. The oath, historically taken by physicians, stipulates that they will do their professional best to administer care regardless of an individual's race, religion, creed, etc. Juxtapose the altruism of the Hippocratic Oath to the oath practiced by self-appointed race-healers. I call it the Hypocritical Oath, and its foundation is based on hypocrisy instead of humanitarianism. These race-healers prescribe and administer grievance-laced placebos to exploit the pre-existing condition of victimhood that's afflicting the black community. In other words, it's the RGI's method of Pavlovian conditioning, and it's difficult to break. Nonetheless, attempting to illuminate the RGI's fallacies to those who've chosen blindness is an exercise in futility.

According to BLM's official website, its members *"affirm that All Black Lives Matter*[31].*"* BLM's affirmation that *"All Black Lives Matter"* absolutely exemplifies the Hypocritical Oath. Clearly, its *"All Black Lives Matter"* motto doesn't apply to the black lives turned into anti-matter by black thugs — which explains why BLM's favorite black people to rally for are the "qualified."

The Qualified

The qualified ones are blacks killed by whites. They're the minority within a minority whose deaths will be praised and remembered more than their lives. Members of this elite club have hit the BLM lottery, and the BLM benefits package includes:

Marches with customized slogans/props   Front page celebrity endorsements

Presidential commentary   Black fraternity covers funeral costs

Eulogy from RGI Member   The Wrath of Khan (Farrakhan)

Parents may speak at the U.N.   Propagandized Mural

One super qualified person may even get a Super Bowl shout out

But wait... the perks don't stop there:

- Canonization with eternal recognition as a martyr despite existing rap sheet
- Incessant comparisons to icons of the Civil Rights movement i.e. Dr. King/Emmett Till
- Foundation created with celebrity endorsements
- Funeral live streamed
- The family gets a settlement and if not, can make money selling paraphernalia. Be warned, a family quarrel may ensue.
- The white perpetrator will be caricatured as a racist demon whose believes that black lives don't matter
- Wikipedia page

The Disqualified

The disqualified ones are blacks killed by blacks. Being murdered sucks, and for these following individuals, it sucked more because the perpetrator was black. Thus, they were disqualified from national temper tantrums on their behalf, #BlackLivesMatter hashtags, or any other BLM race-based grievance benefits. Ultimately, disqualified blacks have to settle for anonymity and simple makeshift rituals (stuffed-animal memorials, and candlelight vigils) reserved for black-on-black homicide victims.

For example, on a Labor Day weekend in Brooklyn, New York, one-year-old Antiq Hennis was shot dead while being pushed in a stroller by his father. The bullet pierced his skull and according to an eyewitness, *"there was blood all over the stroller."* The bullets were intended for the child's father who had an extensive, rap sheet across two states; including weapons possession, controlled substances, automobile theft, and assault. The sins of the father visited his offspring. A stroller march or any march did not occur on the young victim's behalf.

No stroller march for 18-month-old Antiq Hennis shot & killed while in a stroller. Instead, this tribute.

'I shot that motherf****'!: Baby killer's sick boast as he thought he hit the child's father before a witness shouted back 'no you idiot, you shot the kid'
dailymail.co.uk

| Kamiya French | Angel Hooper | Amiracle Williams |

Michigan man kills 2-year-old girl by shooting her execution-style to torture her dad: police

newyorkdailynews.com

[Author's Note: Kamiya was sitting on a porch with her dad when the urban terrorist walked up and shot her point-blank range. His motive was retaliation: telling police that he wanted Kamiya's father to watch her die. The father and a 12-year-old family friend were also shot during this hate crime. Yes, hate crime!]

Girl, 6, killed buying bubblegum in K.C. drive-by shooting

cbsnews.com

[Author's Note: Angel was at a store with her father when she was shot in the head. Hmmm... I wonder why there were no "Bubble Gum" marches. Is it because she wasn't buying Skittles?]

Facebook Fight Led To Fatal Shooting Of 3-Year-Old Amiracle Williams, Detroit Police Say

huffingtonpost.com

[Author's Note: An altercation over Facebook posts occurred outside Amiracle's home when someone took out a machine gun and began to fire repeatedly, striking Amiracle and three family members.]

Chicago

Year after year, Chicago, also known as the "The Second City," places first among U.S cities with the most number of shootings and black homicide victims. Chicago, also called "Chiraq" — due to the war-like conditions in its urban areas being comparable to war-torn Iraq — is brimming with disqualified blacks. To thugs, "Chiraq" is a term of endearment, whereas the RGI thinks the name makes blacks look bad. It's funny how the savages who create those deplorable conditions are never demonized for making blacks look bad. I digress. BLM's website lists twenty-seven chapters[32], but if black lives truly mattered, Chicago should be its headquarters or at least, the biggest and busiest chapter. In short, Chicago — where the son of Mayor Rahm Emanuel was once assaulted and robbed near the mayor's home — is the number one place where black lives splatter via black-on-black genocide.

The Chicago Tribune reported that at least nineteen people were shot and killed New Year's weekend 2016, including a person gunned down just blocks away from the mayor's home — another hundred were shot but survived. Within the first 10 days of 2016, more than a hundred Chicagoans were shot — three times more than 2015. Overall, Chicago's homicides in January's 2016 increased 75 percent compared to January 2015. Moreover, from January to the end of March 2016, there were 677 shooting victims, a staggering 88.5 percent increase from the 359 over the same period in 2015. Chicago's first quarter of this year also saw a 72 percent rise in murders compared to 2015's first quarter. Those 141 Chi-town homicides over three months were more than America's two largest cities (Los Angeles and New York) combined. In response to the nearly 3,000 people shot by the end of 2015, Chicago police spokesman Anthony Guglielmelli released a statement that presently holds true; urban terrorists are the root of the virulent violence.

"So far this year, the majority of the gun violence we've seen are a result of chronic gang conflicts driven in part by social media commentary and petty disputes among rival factions."

Laquan McDonald Qualifies

Out of all the Chicago carnage, unsurprisingly, only one particular death was sexy enough for BLM. Laquan McDonald[33], a 17-year-old black male armed with a 3-inch knife, was shot 16 times by Chicago Police Officer Jason Van Dyke from approximately 10 feet away. Video of the shooting, captured on one police cruiser's dashboard camera, was released to the public 13 months after the incident. Officer Van Dyke was charged with first-degree murder a few hours after the video's release, and hundreds of protesters took to the streets. On the second night of protests, demonstrators tore off lights from a public Christmas tree in Daley Plaza and multiple marchers were arrested. On Black Friday, a major shopping day for retailers, protesters chanted "sixteen shots" and other slogans while marching on Michigan Avenue, Chicago's central shopping district. This caused some businesses to shut their doors and police to close Michigan Avenue — a six-lane street.

Jabari Dean, a 21-year-old college student, posted an online threat to kill 16 unspecified white males — one for every shot fired at McDonald, plus any white police officers who might intervene — at the University of Chicago.

"This is my only warning. At 10 a.m. on Monday mourning (sic) I am going to the campus quad of the University of Chicago. I will be armed with a M-4 Carbine and two Desert Eagles all fully loaded. I will execute aproximately (sic) 16 white male students and or staff, which is the same number of time (sic) McDonald was killed.

I then will die killing any number of white policemen in the process. This is not a joke. I am to do my part and rid the world of the white devils. I expect you to do the same..."

The university canceled classes scheduled for the next day. Dean was summarily arrested by the FBI. Had Dean successfully followed through on his threats, and been subsequently killed by the police, his casket would've received a hero's welcome from BLMers.

Chicago threat suspect allegedly sought to avenge Laquan McDonald's death
cnn.com

Chiraq's Disqualified Blacks

The demise of a child is unnatural, but in Chiraq, it's a way of life. Not only are children killed as collateral damage between urban terrorists, these innocent souls are oftentimes targeted. Children are dying before they reach double-digits in years. Most of us can remember the anticipation and excitement when transitioning from single to double-digit years. I'm not hyperbolizing when stating that I have emails older than many of the kids dying in urban America. These heinous and unfathomable acts should infuriate the masses and are nothing more than examples of adults failing to safeguard the young. Laws exist to protect children from the many forms of abuse — mental, physical, sexual, neglect — but defending our young against lawless predators should be inherent.

Amari Brown

The Windy City, which recorded more murders than any other municipality in 2015, experienced a bloody July Fourth weekend — 11 people killed, more than 50 wounded. One of the weekend's victims was seven-year-old Amari Brown, who police said was killed during a drive-by that was likely intended for his father, a high-ranking gang member. The boy's father had been previously arrested 45 times with 12 convictions and was out on bail at the time of his son's murder. Amari had just returned from watching the holiday fireworks with his family when urban terrorists opened fire at a group of people. His father refused to help detectives with the investigation. Amari's death by a black thug meant disqualification.

7-year-old Amari Brown fatally shot while celebrating 4th of July in Humboldt Park

homicides.suntimes.com

7-year-old Amari Brown

"Hamburger" Smith

Antonio Smith, affectionately called Fat Baby and Hamburger, loved to make other people laugh, his family members recalled. Also, the fourth-grade honor roll student was so smart that he could *"sell water to a whale,"* according to his obituary distributed at the church where he was baptized and sang in the choir. His framed Washington Park peewee football No. 84 jersey stood to the left of his small white casket. His demise was sponsored by urban terrorism.

One afternoon, four urban terrorists were driving around looking to shoot rival gang members when they spotted two foes. Certain that these two were targets, one of the urban terrorists —

already on parole for another gun-related crime — exited the car to approach them on foot. In the process, he came across Antonio Smith who was playing in the rear yard of a residence. Believing that the 9-year-old was yelling a warning to his intended victims, he shot Antonio Smith six times — hitting his right chest, right outside forearm, center back, right lower chest, right shoulder, and left hand, plus two additional graze wounds to the left hand. *"I just hit a shorty. I just hit a shorty,"* was his reaction after hopping into a getaway car. Prosecutors said the shooter also urinated on his hands to cleanse them of gunpowder residue, and then changed his shirt and returned home to comply with his electronic monitoring requirements. Antonio's lifeless body was found on a concrete slab just a few feet from railroad tracks that have long served as the dividing line between the two rival gang factions.

The murder of a 9-year-old boy
chicagotribune.com

Prosecutors: Gunman told fellow gang member 'I just hit a shorty'
chicagotribune.com

Being killed by a gangbanger disqualified "Hamburger"

Tyshawn Lee

The sins of nine-year-old Tyshawn Lee's gang-banging father cost the fourth-grader his young life. According to prosecutors, an urban terrorist — facing five felony charges in three separate cases, including the murder of 19-year-old Brianna Jenkins and the attempted murder of 20-year-old Deshari Bowens[34] — had a vendetta against a rival gang because his brother was killed and mother shot. He vowed to kill *"grandmas, mothers, and children."* So, his gang of urban terrorists went out daily, armed with guns, seeking revenge. Tyshawn, a kid who loved to play basketball, was spotted at a local park. The urban terrorist — who later confessed that he had originally planned to kidnap Tyshawn and cut off his fingers and ears — approached Tyshawn and asked if he wanted to go to the store. Tyshawn responded that he didn't have any money. The thug then stated that he'd buy the fourth-grader whatever he wanted. Tyshawn took the bait, and his green trust cost him his life. As they walked down an alley, Tyshawn was shot execution-style. The basketball he carried was found nearby. Prosecutors say after murdering Tyshawn, the urban terrorist wanted to return to the park and kill all the kids there but police were already present. Showing no remorse, the depraved urban terrorist wrote a rap song bragging about Tyshawn's murder and even described how the 9-year-old suffered from the gunshots. *"Shorty couldn't take it no more. Shorty couldn't take it no more,"* was a verse on the sociopath's song.

McCarthy says 9-year-old boy targeted, lured into alley and executed
chicagotribune.com

PROSECUTORS: SUSPECT IN TYSHAWN LEE MURDER WANTED TO TORTURE BOY, SHOOT UP PARK
abc7chicago.com

Tyshawn's death by a black thug meant disqualification

Memphis

BLM's website states that it *"is working for a world where Black lives are no longer systematically and intentionally targeted for demise[35]."* Well, Memphis is yet another "black" city *"where black lives are systematically and intentionally targeted for demise."* But since the culprits responsible for the demise of blacks aren't exploitable — because they're also black, BLM stays true to its Hypocritical Oath and turns a blind eye.

Placing second on Forbes' *"America's Most Dangerous Cities 2015"* list, and sixth on *NeighborhoodScout.com's* 2016 list of *"Top 100 Most Dangerous Cities in the U.S.,"* the *"Bluff City"* doesn't bluff when it comes to violent crime. More than 98 percent of Tennessee's other communities have a lower crime rate, and one's chances of becoming a victim of either violent or property crime in Memphis are one in 13. Additionally, Neighborhood Scout says that Memphis has the fourth, sixth, and twenty-second most dangerous neighborhoods — #4 E. Mclemore Ave/Latham St, #6 E. Eh Crump Blvd/S 4th St, #22 Thomas St/Frayser Blvd — on its *Top 25 Most Dangerous Neighborhoods in America* list. With a crime index ranking of one out of 100 (100 being the safest), Memphis is only safer than one-percent of American cities. In 2015, 74.5 percent of Memphis' homicide victims were black males, and 68.3 percent were under the age of 35.

Analysis: Homicide victims in Memphis far more likely to be black men
commercialappeal.com

Additionally, *WMC Action News 5* reported that 435 children were shot or shot at in Memphis. The unbelievable amount of young Memphians harmed included 15-year-old Cateria Stokes[36], killed during a drive-by shooting while sleeping, and 7-year-old Kirsten Williams[37], killed less than 24 hours later by a drive-by shooting as she played with friends in a neighbor's driveway. Many locals believe that seven-year-old Kirsten's death was retaliation for Cateria's death. Despite the 435 children being shot or shot at in Memphis, BLM sits on its hands waiting for, a martyr moment which none of these kids qualified.

435 children shot, shot at in Memphis during 2015
wmcactionnews5.com

7-year-old Kirsten Williams & 15-year-old Cateria Stokes' funerals were held on the same day

Memphis, like most majority-black cities, has a history of using misdirection and scapegoating as a means of addressing its self-inflicted ailments. Young black males are far more likely to be the victims of homicide here than any other race or gender. But, instead of changing its bloody reality, Memphis politicians want to change people's perception of Memphis. Hence, the banning of a popular, nationally televised show that inadvertently exposed Memphis' dark side. Memphis Commercial Appeal reported:

Elected officials aren't generally known for their camera-shyness. Yet some Memphis City Council members weren't comfortable with local police appearing on a documentary series called "The First 48."

The series, which airs on the A&E cable channel, follows detectives as they try to solve murders within the first two days after the crimes have been committed.

Council member Wanda Halbert said the show was giving viewers elsewhere around the country a bad impression of Memphis.

"I heard out-of-town people say Memphis was out of control," Halbert said. "We were exposing the world to the worst aspects of our city."

The show actually highlighted the amount of time, effort, and sacrifices that Memphis' detectives dedicate to solving homicides. The public, especially where the "no-snitching" mantra is law, has a behind-the-scene access to a thankless but necessary job. Understanding how detectives operate can potentially help to build a bridge between police and community. Seemingly, the city council prefers a rift instead of a bridge — even instituting a 4.6 percent pay cut for the Memphis Police Department. The police union responded by sponsoring billboards that warned, *"DANGER: Enter at your own risk; This city does not support public safety."* The former mayor, A C Wharton, blamed the billboards for hurting Memphis' image instead of the true source — urban terrorism and the liberal policies that enable it.

Memphis police cut ties with TV's 'First 48': Show sensationalizes city violence, council says
commercialappeal.com

Memphis mayor says police union's 'danger' billboards hurting city's image
foxnews.com

Memphis Police Association put up billboards

In a sensible piece titled, *"Fiddling Away the Future[38],"* Dr. Walter E. Williams — a John M. Olin Distinguished Professor of Economics at George Mason University — questioned the motives of Memphis' mayor A C Wharton:

What about Memphis Mayor A C Wharton's proposal to "help" his black constituents? He has proposed to dig up the bodies of Confederate Gen. Nathan Bedford Forrest and his wife and remove them from a city park. One wonders whether he thinks marshaling resources to do that is more important than dealing with the city's 145 murders, 320 rapes, 6,900 aggravated assault calls, and 3,000 robberies. All of the Memphis black homicide victims were murdered by other blacks.

Laughably, the mayor's plan to bring Memphis back from the brink of destruction is by demonizing white people — dead white people at that. Such a maneuver has solidified A C Wharton as one BLM's favorite mayors. After all, they share the same inaction plan.

Memphis mayor: Dig up dead Confederate general, wife
examiner.com

Ferguson, Missouri Memory

Every time Ferguson is referenced, I automatically think of that young black kid's senseless murder. Shot and killed while being in the right place at the right time was truly a tragedy. After all, she was shot and killed while doing homework at home. And according to her mother, nine-year-old Jamyla Bolden was usually the first to yell, *"Mom, they're shooting,"* whenever neighborhood gunshots erupted. However, this round of gunfire didn't give Jamyla a chance to warn others or even take cover. Oh wait, you do know that other homicides — besides "the one" — occurred in Ferguson... right?

The fact that most readers may have initially believed that I was referencing Ferguson's *Only Begotten* homicide (Mike Brown), shows the success of BLM's Hypocritical Oath. Both Jamyla Bolden and Mike Brown were two Ferguson natives shot dead; one was a child while the other was depicted as a child. Yet, protesters only chanted, *"Hands up, don't shoot"* for one of them. The *"Hands up, don't shoot"* story has been debunked by the Department of Justice headed by Eric Holder, who arrived in Missouri after Mike Brown's death and declared, *"I am the attorney general of the United States, but I am also a black man[39]."* Furthermore, Holder dispatched dozens of the department's most experienced investigators to Ferguson searching specifically for possible violations of federal criminal civil rights statutes. For the record, no one violates civil rights more than black thugs do, but I digress. Interviews with witnesses and other residents were conducted, and Holder assured, *"I'm confident that through the ability of these people that we'll be able to make a determination of whether or not any federal statutes have in fact been violated[40]. "* Ultimately, the DoJ's report found that Brown's rights were not violated, and it even addressed the incessant *"Hands up, don't shoot"* narrative:

"Although there are several individuals who have stated that Brown held his hands up in an unambiguous sign of surrender prior to Wilson shooting him dead, their accounts do not support a prosecution of Wilson. As detailed throughout this report, some of those accounts are inaccurate because they are inconsistent with the physical and forensic evidence; some of those accounts are materially inconsistent with that witness's own prior statements with no explanation, credible for otherwise, as to why those accounts changed over time. Certain other witnesses who originally stated Brown had his hands up in surrender recanted their original accounts, admitting that they did not witness the shooting or parts of it, despite what they initially reported either to federal or local law enforcement or to the media. Prosecutors did not rely on those accounts when making a prosecutive decision. While credible witnesses gave varying accounts of exactly what Brown was doing with his hands as he moved toward Wilson – i.e., balling them, holding them out, or pulling up his pants up – and varying accounts of how he was moving – i.e., "charging," moving in "slow motion," or "running" – they all establish that Brown was moving toward Wilson when Wilson shot him. Although some witnesses state that Brown held his hands up at shoulder level with his palms facing outward for a brief moment, these same witnesses describe Brown then dropping his hands and "charging" at Wilson."

Feelings > Facts

The *"Hands up, don't shoot"* tale has been dismantled to a point where even the left-leaning Washington Post added it to its annual list of shame, *"The biggest Pinocchios of 2015"*:

"This phrase became a rallying cry for protests after the fatal shooting of a black 18-year-old by a white police officer, Darren Wilson. Witness accounts spread after the shooting that Michael Brown had his hands raised in surrender, mouthing the words "Don't shoot" as his last words before being shot execution-style. Democratic lawmakers raised their hands in solidarity on the House floor. But various investigations concluded this did not happen — and that Wilson acted out of self-defense and was justified in killing Brown"

Instead of *"Hands up, don't shoot,"* the more fitting phrase is, *"Assault a cop, he'll shoot!"* But since the Hypocritical Oath maintains the lie of victimhood, *"Hands up, don't shoot"* will continue to be propagated and recited as if it's gospel. In fact, the apt line, *"When the legend becomes fact, print the legend,"* (from the 1962 classic western film *The Man Who Shot Liberty Valance*) is essentially the mission statement of today's black press. The Ferguson fib is printed as Ferguson fact.

The biggest Pinocchios of 2015
washingtonpost.com

Jamyla Bolden's death yielded no demands that city officials step down, the resignation of the entire department, or tribute from the St. Louis Rams football team. Moreover, no self-described "urban militia[41]" offered a cash bounty for her killer's location as was the case for Officer Darren Wilson's whereabouts. However, a protest occurred the night following her death. Unfortunately, it wasn't for her; it was directed at the police for shooting and killing eighteen-year-old Mansur Ball-Bey[42] — a black male — during a drug raid. According to the police, two suspects attempted to escape when officers arrived with a search warrant. Ball-Bey reportedly turned around and pointed his weapon at the officers. He was shot four times. The other suspect got away. Ball-Bey had a stolen gun, and the police retrieved three more guns and an unspecified amount of crack cocaine at the house. The officers who shot him are white. Demonstrators in nearby St. Louis took to the streets, threw rocks and bottles at the police (who arrived with riot gear and armored vehicles) and set fire to a car, vacant house, along with mattresses set out as makeshift barricades. Noteworthy is the fact that Jamyla's house is one block away from where Mike Brown was shot.

Michael Brown (Qualified)   Jamyla Bolden (Disqualified)

Cleveland's Castaway

Cleveland, often referred to locally as "The North Coast," is a majority-black city, and thus, infiltrated by urban terrorism. One's chances of becoming a victim of either violent or property crime in Cleveland are one in 15. Within Ohio, more than 99 percent of the communities have a lower crime rate than Cleveland. Furthermore, Cleveland's crime index of two (100 being the highest) means that it's safer than only two percent of U.S. cities. Because of its rampant criminality, Cleveland has secured the twenty-third spot on *NeighborhoodScout.com's "Top 100 Most Dangerous Cities in the U.S.A."*

The shooting of 12-year-old Tamir Rice[43] occurred in Cleveland after two police officers responded to a dispatch call *"of a male black sitting on a swing and pointing a gun at people"* in a city park. A caller stated that a male was pointing *"a pistol"* at random people in the Cudell Recreation Center. The responding officers reported that Rice reached towards a gun in his waistband upon their arrival, which caused them to shoot at Rice. He died the following day. The gun was fake but the ensuing protests were real. Tamir Rice's death qualified for the BLM benefits package. Additionally, the Smithsonian National Museum of African-American History and Culture is seeking to have the gazebo (where he was killed) preserved[44]. Five-year-old Ramon Burnett was also shot and killed in Cleveland, but for obvious reasons his death wasn't as scintillating to the RGI or BLM. As reported by *Cleveland.com*:

Ramon Burnett's Labor Day weekend started out as typical as any end-of-summer celebration for a 5-year-old boy.

The kindergartner at George Washington Carver Elementary School, known to friends and family as "Dink," came to his grandmother's apartment on Louise Harris Drive after school Friday afternoon.

He used his heartwarming smile to score a quarter from a family friend. He traded it with a neighbor for a homemade slushy. He tossed a football with the neighborhood children in a yard behind his grandmother's home. Parents watched from their stoops and through the open doors.

Then came the gunshots.

At 5 p.m., with the sun still shining, Ramon became the youngest victim in a season punctuated by violence in what is becoming one of the bloodiest summers in Cleveland in nearly a decade.

When officers arrived, they found the boy lying next to the football that he tossed around with friends. There, the boy who loved Spiderman and whose mother called him "handsome" would draw some of his last breaths.

5-year-old tossing football becomes latest casualty in Cleveland's deadly summer

cleveland.com

One was shot while holding a football... the other was shot while holding a toy gun. Two tragedies, but only one qualified for martyrdom

Only Oscar is Oscar-Worthy

In Oakland, which is number three on Forbes 2015 list of *"America's Most Dangerous Cities"* and number nine on NeighborhoodScout's list of *"100 Most Dangerous Cities in the U.S.,"* exists a one in 13 chance of becoming a victim of either violent or property crime. Additionally, more than 99% of California's other communities have a lower crime rate than Oakland, whose West Oakland section has the fifteenth most dangerous neighborhood in America. Oakland's crime index of one (100 being the safest) means that it's safer than only one percent of U.S. cities, and that harrowing statistic isn't because of the police.

In 2009, 22-year-old Oscar Grant[45] was fatally shot while handcuffed by a white BART (Bay Area Rapid Transit) police officer. BART settled with Grant's daughter and mother for a total of $2.8 million in 2011. The incident was the basis of the critically acclaimed 2013 film *Fruitvale Station[46]*, which grossed more than seventeen million dollars worldwide from an initial budget of $900,000.

But there's another Fruitvale story, and I'm not talking about the sequel to Fruitvale Station. The star of this Fruitvale story is a little girl who would've been a third-grader at Fruitvale Elementary School, but instead had her fate determined by an urban terrorist. Eight-year-old Alaysha Carradine, whose family affectionately referred to as Ladybug, was shot and killed at her best friend's sleepover. An urban terrorist rang the apartment's doorbell and started shooting as Alaysha's friend opened the door. The bullets pierced the apartment's metal gate and struck four of the five people inside. Alaysha was killed. Her seven-year-old best friend sustained wounds that weren't life-threatening, as did her friend's four-year-old brother and 64-year-old grandmother. Alaysha was the youngest of Oakland's murder victims in 2013.

Oakland 8-year-old shot dead at sleepover
mercurynews.com

Oscar Grant's death qualified him for a movie while Alaysha Carradine's death didn't even qualify her for a special on BET. Consequently, her story remains untold to the masses.

Both shot & killed, but only one story appealed to moviemakers

The Black Press

If you watch the black press to learn about the state of affairs in the black community, you'll be informed; if you believe the black press about the state of affairs in the black community you'll be misinformed. That's because the black press — anchored by the National Association of Black Journalists (NABJ) — is the official mouthpiece of the RGI, and thus, only speaks on the behalf of the "qualified."

The National Association of Black Journalists' constitution[47]:

"We, the members of the National Association of Black Journalists, who are striving for credible journalism that comprehensively portrays the voices and experiences of African Americans and people from the black diaspora for a society and world that values them..."

In short, the NABJ places emphasis on everything black except black violence and criminality. Therefore, it practices the Hypocritical Oath. It is standard operating procedure to racialize black issues, and the so-called "black" websites — Black Voices, owned by the Huffington Post, The Grio, owned by MSNBC, The Root.com, owned by the Washington Post — are the heaviest promoters of the victimization narrative. Since employment is fickle in the media field, stories about victimhood receive top billing because they generate high web traffic, which translates into job security. Ebony, a financially-struggling black magazine, once started a *"Save Our Boys"* campaign, as if blacks are being slaughtered by whites. As far as black-on-black violence coverage, the black press is lackadaisical, yet holds the mainstream media to a standard that it doesn't hold itself.

Essence's Black Lives Matter edition only featured "qualified" blacks

#BlackTwitter

#BlackTwitter is the social media arm of the RGI and essentially, an extension of the black press. In fact, the NABJ and Columbia University Graduate School of Journalism hosted a Black Twitter Conference to consolidate the agendas of the black press and #BlackTwitter. According to Salon.com, #BlackTwitter is the *"new underground railroad,"* a *"collective of active, primarily African-American Twitter users who have created a virtual community ... [and are] proving adept at bringing about a wide range of sociopolitical changes."* Blacks are Twitter's biggest demographic[48] — 28 percent, compared to 20 percent of white, non-Hispanic Americans — and thus, Black Twitter's impact is significant. It uses hashtags to make black topics go viral, create martyrs of the moment, and construct racial grievances. Black Twitter was credited with having stopped a proposed book deal between a Seattle literary agent and one of the jurors in the trial of George Zimmerman. It was also instrumental in a boycott against Paula Deen — a celebrity chef, accused of racism — and affiliated companies and sponsors. In short, #BlackTwitter is a collective of aggrieved armchair activists, hashtag-tivists, and keyboard-kamikazes. There isn't a black grievance that #BlackTwitter doesn't attempt to make viral.

The Secret Power Of Black Twitter
buzzfeed.com

Is Twitter the underground railroad of activism?
salon.com
[Author's Note: Unlike #BlackTwitter, I use my twitter page (@TaleebStarkes) to highlight stories of innocent people killed by urban terrorists.]

The National Association of Black Journalists Presents

THE #BLACKTWITTER

CONFERENCE

2016 NABJ Media Institute - #BlackTwitter16

Saturday, Feb. 27, 2016
Columbia University Graduate School of Journalism
2950 Broadway (at 116th Street)
New York, NY 10027
9 a.m. - 5 p.m.

For more information and registration please visit NABJ.org

Black Press = Black Twitter

Do the Right (RGI) Thing?

When Spike Lee used his #BlackTwitter privilege to retweet an assumed address of George Zimmerman, the intent was clear; Jorge the "white Hispanic" had to suffer for shooting and killing Trayvon Martin. Spike wanted vigilante justice. However, the address he tweeted to his quarter of a million followers actually belonged to a blameless, elderly couple in Sanford, Florida. As a result, their home was bombarded with threats and vitriol aimed at Zimmerman. Lee later apologized and claimed that it was a mistake. The apology wasn't enough. The seniors eventually filed a lawsuit[49] against Spike Lee for placing them in imminent danger. In Lee's reality, the mistake wasn't the tweet itself, but tweeting the wrong address. He never shows this level of passion when it comes to vigilante justice for kids killed by urban terrorists. And that's because the criminal element has handcuffed itself to the black community with the black community's consent. Blacks have the key to uncuff the criminal subculture but refuse to use it.

More evidence that the RGI only fights for the qualified blacks

Bait Master

The black press purports to represent black interests and dialogue, but hesitate to tackle the most pressing issue facing blacks: intraracial genocide. Since 1980, blacks have accounted for almost half of the nation's homicide victims (47.4 percent) and more than half of the offenders (52.4 percent) while only being 13 percent of America's population[50]. The offending rate for blacks is seven times higher than for whites and the victimization rate six times higher. Homicide[51] is the number one cause of death for black males between the ages of 15-34. From 1993 to 2010, black males ages 18 to 24 had the highest rates of firearm homicides[52]. Blacks are eight times more likely to be murdered than whites, and black males are 10 times more likely to be murdered than white males. Even though the offender will be a black person ninety-plus percent of the time, black propaganda states otherwise.

'Black-ish' delves into 'Black Lives Matter' with police brutality episode
newsday.com

A Tuskegee Institute study[53] of all known lynchings of blacks that occurred between 1882-1968. During this 86-year span, which is essentially the post-Civil War era up to the Civil Rights era, 3,446 blacks were reportedly lynched. Presently, black-on-black murder eclipses the number of blacks lynched (over the course of 8 decades) roughly every six months[54].

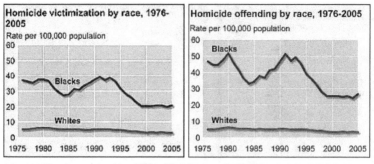

The minority report

Baltimore's 2015 ended as its bloodiest and deadliest year — on a per-capita basis[55]. In 2014, Detroit's police chief called upon law-abiding citizens to take arms against its burgeoning, violent, criminal subculture[56]. And since the black press is quick to point out that violence is typically intraracial, why would it then shift the blame for the continuous urban carnage on racism? Agenda...Agenda...Agenda!

July 1973 Racial Truth < January 2013 Racial Agenda

Along with the black press, apologists (in general) justify the endemic violence in majority-black cities by citing the fact that crimes are largely intraracial. However, the severity of black criminality is unintentionally highlighted when a majority white city like Pittsburgh (Pennsylvania), often named as a *most livable city,"* has the twelfth most dangerous neighborhood in America[57]. This unsafe neighborhood that made the shameful list isn't a white, trailer park neighborhood — it's a black neighborhood. In fact, America's most dangerous cities are never ones dominated by trailer parks, only projects and subsidized housing. In 2014, 85 percent of Pittsburgh homicides were black, specifically, young black men — including collateral damage victims. In this majority white city, shouldn't white people be the bulk of the homicides? After all, white people commit crimes too, white-on-white homicides occur too — as I'm often reminded. Blacks are approximately 25 percent of Pittsburgh's population, and Pittsburgh's Police Chief Cameron McLay told Publicsource.org, *"There's a victimology here that is completely unacceptable."* The police chief also acknowledged that police and the community had become acclimated to violence. Publicsource.org reported further:

"In Pittsburgh, only certain neighborhoods bleed.

PublicSource.org mapped every homicide in the city from 2010 through 2015. The results show a startling geographic division — and clear racial disparity — in who suffers the brunt of the violence.

There were no killings in Shady Side. None in Point Breeze, where some of the city's wealthiest residents make their homes.

In fact, there were no murders at all in the huge area — mostly white and affluent — south of Penn Avenue down to Interstate 376. The murder-free zone runs from the eastern city limit up to the borders of Bloomfield and Oakland.

But from Penn Avenue and above — in East Hills, Homewood, Larimer, Lincoln-Lemington-Belmar and the northern part of East Liberty — there were 94 homicides during that six-year period. More than half remain unsolved.

Again, that's nearly 100 murders on one side of the street, and zero on the other.

The Hill District had 42 homicides. More than half remain unsolved."

Police attribute the violence to very few individuals, and it doesn't take Columbo to determine the race of the perpetrators. Moreover, if the perps were white with black victims, the unsolved murder cases would likely be zero. Unquestionably, the community would be actively involved.

In Pittsburgh, neighborhood violence lives next door to prosperity
publicsource.org

Wilkinsburg — a poverty-stricken, mostly blighted 66 percent black suburb near Pittsburgh, known for drug trafficking and violence — experienced an incident that's familiar to its bigger sibling. Two urban terrorists methodically shot and killed six people, including a nearly eight-month-pregnant woman and her fetus, at a backyard cookout. Investigators said one gunman fired from an alley near the backyard party, which prompted the partygoers to run toward a house for cover, where they were ambushed by another rifle-wielding gunman. The police have desperately urged witnesses or anyone with information to come forward. Meanwhile, the black press showed no interest in this tragedy until a white Pittsburgh anchorwoman said something provocative that the RGI could exploit as racism. The anchorwoman posted this truthful commentary (in part) on her Facebook account:

> You needn't be a criminal profiler to draw a mental sketch of the killers who broke so many hearts two weeks ago Wednesday. I will tell you they live within 5 miles of Franklin Avenue and Ardmore Boulevard and have been hiding out since in a home likely much closer to that backyard patio than anyone thinks. They are young black men, likely teens or in their early 20s. They have multiple siblings from multiple fathers and their mothers work multiple jobs. These boys have been in the system before. They've grown up there. They know the police. They've been arrested. They've made the circuit and nothing has scared them enough. Now they are lost. Once you kill a neighbor's three children, two nieces and her unborn grandson, there's no coming back. There's nothing nice to say about that.

All of sudden, RGI splinter groups that I had never known existed showed up to feign outrage. Groups such as The Pittsburgh Black Media Federation, who issued a statement[58] that read, in part:

"The irresponsible statements demonstrate a persistent problem with how African-Americans are negatively stereotyped by too many journalists and news organizations."

Unsurprisingly, there was more outrage about the Emmy-winning reporter's words than the actions of the urban terrorists. Noticeably, no one disputed her assessment, only her *"white privilege"* for giving license to her observation. I bet that none of the "concerned" grievance groups contributed to the burial fund of the victims. Meanwhile, the anchor — under pressure from the PC police — retracted her comments, apologized, and then fell onto her sword; all for the delight of the RGI. Ultimately, none of her exhibited remorse mattered; she was fired. Her 18 years on air and accumulation of 21 regional Emmy awards meant nothing in this age of political correctness. Refer to the *"Land of the Free, Home of the Offended"* chapter.

Pittsburgh anchor regrets 'insensitive' post on black shooting suspects
wkbn.com

Black-on-black genocide is so common that in a rare moment of honesty, the New Pittsburgh Courier openly celebrated when June of 2013 yielded no Black homicides. It rejoiced:

"The past few weeks have been loaded with news, with the most popular being the Supreme Court decisions on Affirmative Action, Voting Rights and Gay Marriages. But there was an even bigger news story that occurred that most of the media missed. It was huge. No Black homicides in the month of June. Yes you read it right. No Black homicides in the entire month of June. Zero."

Just Sayin'...No Black homicides in June
newpittsburghcourieronline.com

Although Pittsburgh (called the "Steel City" because of its many steel-related businesses) lost its steel industries, unemployment didn't cause it to sink into a dystopia as Detroit did. Pittsburgh, also known as "the City of Bridges," is yet another place that the RGI will use as a bridge into victimhood while burning the bridge to accountability.

BLM's Favorite Doctor

If BLM had a primary care physician, it would be Dr. Kermit Gosnell. Like BLM, he practiced the Hypocritical Oath. Although "women's health" was professedly the primary focus of his Women's Medical Health Society clinic in Philadelphia, the clinic actually focused on the health of profits. Over three decades, Dr. Gosnell made millions of dollars performing thousands of dangerous abortions, many of them illegal late-term procedures. Dubbed as "The House of Horrors," his clinic had no trained nurses or medical staff other than Gosnell — a family physician not certified in obstetrics or gynecology. Dr. Gosnell's practice accommodated women who were "too pregnant" and couldn't get abortions elsewhere. Under Pennsylvania law, abortions are illegal after 24 weeks of pregnancy and most doctors won't perform procedures after 20 weeks because of the high health risks. Dr. Gosnell, on the other hand, interpreted this high risk as high reward. The bigger the baby, the more he charged. He didn't advertise, but word got around. He had cornered this niche market. Women came from across the city, state, and region for illegal late-term abortions; paying $325 for first-trimester abortions and $1,600 to $3,000 for abortions up to thirty weeks. The clinic took in $10,000 to $15,000 a day, authorities said.[59]

The grand jury report stated that he regularly delivered live, viable babies in the third trimester of pregnancy and then murdered these newborns by severing their spinal cords with scissors. Sometimes, Gosnell even joked about the babies, saying one was so large he could... *"walk me to the bus stop."*

Philadelphia's District Attorney detailed the clinic's environment:

"When the team members entered the clinic, they were appalled, describing it to the Grand Jury as 'filthy,' 'deplorable,' 'disgusting,' 'very unsanitary, very outdated, horrendous,' and 'by far, the worst' that these experienced investigators had ever encountered. There was blood on the floor. A stench of urine filled the air. A flea-infested cat was wandering through the facility, and there were cat feces on the stairs. Semi-conscious women scheduled for abortions were moaning in the waiting room or the recovery room, where they sat on dirty recliners covered with blood-stained blankets. All the women had been sedated by unlicensed staff – long before Gosnell arrived at the clinic – and staff members could not accurately state what medications or dosages they had administered to the waiting patients. Many of the medications in inventory were past their expiration dates... surgical procedure rooms were filthy and unsanitary... resembling 'a bad gas station restroom.' Instruments were not sterile. Equipment was rusty and outdated. Oxygen equipment was covered with dust, and had not been inspected. The same corroded suction tubing used for abortions was the only tubing available for oral airways if assistance for breathing was needed.

[F]etal remains [were] haphazardly stored throughout the clinic– in bags, milk jugs, orange juice cartons, and even in cat-food containers... Gosnell admitted to Detective Wood that at least 10 to 20 percent... were probably older than 24 weeks [the legal limit]... In some instances, surgical incisions had been made at the base of the fetal skulls. The investigators found a row of jars containing just the severed feet of fetuses. In the basement, they discovered medical waste piled high. The intact 19-week fetus delivered by Mrs. Mongar three months earlier was in a freezer. In all, the remains of 45 fetuses were recovered ... at least two of them, and probably three, had been viable."

Baby remains were stuffed into cabinets, jars, bags, plastic jugs, freezers, and the basement for no medical purposes. One witness said a sink was plunged and a baby's arm came out. Another report said a toilet had to be removed when a baby became lodged in a pipe.

In addition to performing illegal abortions, Dr. Gosnell ran an illegal pill mill. The doctor of death is currently serving life plus 30 years.

DA: WEST PHILADELPHIA ABORTION DOCTOR KILLED 7 BABIES WITH SCISSORS
6abc.com

Trial of abortion doctor Kermit Gosnell reveals 'a house of horrors'
thelead.blogs.cnn.com

Despite the serial killing of babies, and massive amount of blood Gosnell had on his hands, the RGI conveniently looked the other way. However, another notable black doctor, who happens to be a retired neurosurgeon, staunchly pro-life, and practitioner of the Hippocratic Oath wasn't extended the blind eye treatment. This doctor is Dr. Ben Carson, and he was called a coon on social media by RGI member Anthea Butler. Interestingly, Gosnell has yet to be called a coon for what he did for more than thirty years but Dr. Ben Carson was name-called because his racial authenticity wasn't validated by the self-appointed gatekeepers of "blackness." Such is the state of affairs in the black community. Anthea Butler, a black Ivy League professor and Black Lives Matter supporter tweeted[60], *"If only there was a 'coon of the year' award,"* in response to Dr. Ben Carson's belief that people have the right to display Confederate flags on private property.

ProfB
@AntheaButler

@goldietaylor If only there was a "coon of the year" award...

9/29/15, 10:18 AM

Grievance professor's comment about Dr. Carson

Black professors such as Walter E. Williams and Thomas Sowell are also likely considered coons since they're not RGI stockholders. However, the irony is that Dr. Carson saved people whereas Dr. Gosnell killed people, babies specifically. Even so, Gosnell was never called a coon or anything close to the derogative term. The RGI consistently supports black killers of blacks, regardless of the victim's age or stage of life.

One doctor practiced the Hippocratic Oath while the other practiced the Hypocritical Oath

Chapter IV

Fifty Shades of Gray... Freddie Gray

"We must reject the idea that every time a law's broken, society is guilty rather than the lawbreaker. It is time to restore the American precept that each individual is accountable for his actions." – Ronald Reagan

With 2015 being a record year for homicides, shootings, and overall violence in Baltimore, the "Charm City" is undoubtedly losing its charm. Nowadays, it's "Harm City." Nearly 90 percent of its homicides occurred via shootings, and the nonfatal shootings skyrocketed more than 75 percent from 2014. In a reactionary move, the cash-strapped city contemplated investing in ShotSpotter[61] — an expensive technology system designed to detect and pinpoint gunfire leading to quicker police response — but reneged saying deployment would put a strain on other crime-fighting resources. Officials say the problem is "gun violence," when actually the problem is "violent people with guns violence." Which is why Baltimore's 2015 crime spike was unparalleled among the 30 largest U.S. cities. There were 40 homicides in May, 29 more in June, and then 45 in July — a record. Not only did Baltimore — America's twenty-sixth largest city, whose population is roughly 622,000 — match the homicide count of America's most populous city New York — whose population is approximately 8.4 million — it unbelievably doubled New York City's violent crime rate. Unsurprisingly, Baltimore is a mainstay on *Forbes* top ten list of *"America's Most Dangerous Cities,"* and NeighborhoodScout's lists of *"Top 30 Highest Murder Rate Cities in the U.S."* and *"Top 100 Most Dangerous Cities in the U.S."* With its one in 16 chance of becoming a victim of either violent or property crime, *NeighborhoodScout.com* gave Baltimore a crime index ranking of three out of 100 (100 being the safest), which means that Baltimore is considered safer than only three percent of American cities. Adding insult to injury, Baltimore is home to two of the worst neighborhoods in the country, according to *NeighborhoodScout.com*. W. Mulberry St./N. Fremont Ave. is the nation's worst neighborhood and Druid Hill Ave./ Laurens St. is the seventh worst. One's chances of being victimized in those areas are one in 11 and one in 12 respectively. Even the white hipsters have to consider those odds before gentrification.

Realize that 2015's record-setting violence, carnage, and dysfunction occurred in a 63 percent black city with blacks occupying the top positions — including a black congressman. Hundreds of black lives were extinguished by the same melaninated menaces, yet; only one black life mattered above all. And flags in the hood will forever fly at half-mast in his memory: Freddie Gray, the fairest victim of them all.

Deadliest year in Baltimore history ends with 344 homicides
baltimoresun.com

Baltimore = Kryptonite

The Folk Hero

Once upon a time in Baltimore, an angel — personified as a man — dwelled amongst the urbanites. The urbanites were a tribe indigenous to Baltimore and many other American inner-cites. The urbanites clashed with the enforcers. The enforcers were a tribe who wore blue uniforms and enforced a code of conduct that was conducive for a civilized society to thrive. Because the urbanites observed their own set of laws, they had enmity towards the enforcers for their law enforcement ways. However, not all members of the urbanite tribe were rebellious, but those who weren't rebellious usually protected the urbanites that were rebellious and even made excuses for their fellow tribesmen's transgressions. In other words, the sheep protected the wolves. The angel who dwelled amongst the urbanites was one of those defiant tribesmen, and repeatedly violated the laws that governed civilized society. When discovered by the enforcers, they apprehended and allegedly crucified him for all to see. After his crucifixion, the urbanites were restless. As a result, the civilization that the enforcers zealously protected immediately felt the wrath of his tribe. Civilized society was turned inside out; the urbanites shaped the city into their image and likeness — which is what the angel who appeared in the form of a man wanted all along. The End.

Folklore Ends, Truth Begins

BLM paints Freddie Gray in one shade: victim. However, this young man's lengthy rap sheet (20 cases, with five pending when he died) revealed the other shade: career criminal. Despite the fact that he was urban cancer, his alleged demise by cop was an automatic qualification for the BLM benefits package — which included sanitization of his image and life. Dr. Jamal Bryant, pastor of a Baltimore mega-church, and prominent member of the black clergy led the charge to propagate the romanticized narrative of Freddie Gray. Pastor Bryant declared[62], *"Freddie Gray is a symbol for so many of us in this city and in this community of what it means to be a young black man, trying to fight up against what seems to be insurmountable odds."* So, according to the Pastor, Freddie Gray is a symbol. A symbol? A symbol like the artist formerly known as Prince? Oh, so that's why the drug dealer formerly known as Freddie Gray is BLM's symbol (This would be funny if it weren't true). In reality, Freddie Gray is simply a symbol of the occupational hazards associated with drug-dealing, and the black community's unwillingness to dispose of its garbage. BLM cites his death as an example of a supposed endemic problem of police brutality in the city, but a cursory view of 2015's crime demonstrates that the city isn't suffering from police brutality; it's suffering from criminal brutality. Even after his death in April 2015, homicides topped 30 or 40 a month for five of the next eight months. At year's end, Baltimore had averaged more than a killing a day, with more than 90 percent of the victims being black males and more than half between the ages of 18 and 30. Hey, Pastor, had Freddie Gray been killed by a black hand like the other 90 percent of victims, what would've he symbolized then? Nothing, except the usual apathy and hypocrisy, expressed towards black victims of black perpetrators.

- *3/20/15: Possession of a Controlled Dangerous Substance with intent to distribute, violation of probation*
- *3/3/15:   Malicious destruction of property, second-degree assault*
- *1/20/15: Fourth-degree burglary, trespassing*
- *1/14/15: Possession of a controlled dangerous substance, possession of a controlled dangerous substance with intent to distribute*
- *1/31/14: Possession of narcotics with intent to distribute*
- *12/14/14: Possession of a controlled dangerous substance*
- *1/31/14: Illegal gambling, trespassing*
- *1/25/14: Possession of marijuana*
- *1/28/13: Distribution of narcotics, unlawful possession of a controlled dangerous substance, second-degree assault, second-degree escape*
- *1/13/12: Possession of a controlled dangerous substance with intent to distribute, unlawful possession of a controlled dangerous substance, violation of probation*
- *1/16/08: Possession of a controlled dangerous substance, possession with intent to distribute*
- *1/28/08: Unlawful possession of a controlled dangerous substance*
- *3/14/08: Possession of a controlled dangerous substance with intent to manufacture and distribute*
- *2/11/08: Unlawful possession of a controlled dangerous substance, possession of a controlled dangerous substance*
- *8/29/07: Possession of a controlled dangerous substance with intent to distribute*
- *8/28/07: Possession of marijuana*
- *8/23/07: False statement to a peace officer, unlawful possession of a controlled dangerous substance*
- *7/16/07: Possession of a controlled dangerous substance with intent to distribute, unlawful possession of a controlled dangerous substance (2 counts)*

During my brief human experience, I've learned that fallibility is a prerequisite of our existence: accept the flaws and grow from them. I did and will continue to do so. With that said, Gray's rap sheet illustrates that the only thing he changed was arrest dates.

Criminal Haven

The Sandtown-Winchester/Harlem Park area of Baltimore where Freddie Gray lived and operated his pharmaceutical enterprise is a criminal haven; a petri dish of lawlessness. Its homicide rate is actually higher than Baltimore's homicide rate, so even by B-more's subterranean quality of life standards; Sandtown-Winchester/Harlem Park is ground zero. It's another hood where police have to deal with career criminals who know their lawful rights better than their unlawful wrongs. It's an area where *"disrespect"* led to 17 shots to the body and one to the head of 27-seven-year-old Gregory McFadden. The Baltimore City Health Department found that residents of Sandtown-Winchester/Harlem Park were more than twice as likely to be killed than Baltimore residents overall, and that same ratio exists with nonfatal shootings. Due to its astronomical crime rate, cops are disproportionately engaged there, thus creating the phenomenon of Sandtown-Winchester/Harlem Park having the most residents in state prison than any other census tract in Maryland. Additionally, those 458 inmates cost the state $17 million a year to incarcerate according to the Justice Policy Institute and Prison Policy Initiative. Freddie Gray's alleged nickel ride incident cost taxpayers 6.4 million in settlement money by itself. Even so, whether dead or alive, criminals are costing society more than they're worth.

Report: Sandtown-Winchester leads state in number of people incarcerated
baltimoresun.com

The insanity of Baltimore's 'disrespect' killings
articles.baltimoresun.com

Mum is The Word

During the Baltimore tsunami that followed Freddie Gray's death, and caused millions in damages[63], many people were surprised with Mayor Rawlings-Blake's decision to grant the rioters/looters space to destroy. She stated, *"[w]e also gave those who wished to destroy space to do that as well. And we worked very hard to keep that balance and to put ourselves in the best position to de-escalate[64]."* Her acquiescence wasn't surprising. After all, the mayor simply responded to the criminality in the traditional manner the black community does for its violent subculture — give them space... our space. However, it was surprising that she publically acknowledged the tactic because the black community is usually mum about its non-disclosure agreement with its criminals. The homicide rate in urban America is as high as the national debt because no-snitching is a way of life. If one wants to learn "how to get away with murder," there's no need to watch the television show of the same name; instead, go to Baltimore. Marilyn Mosby, the black State's Attorney, called Baltimore the *"home of witness intimidation, where the 'Stop Snitching' mentality began[65]."* Even with the abundance of surveillance cameras, and advancement of forensic science, detectives hold steadfast that witnesses are the most significant component in successfully bringing charges against a suspect. Although Baltimore police have identified hundreds of shooting suspects in 2015, the lack of community tips has led to few arrests. Consequently, the rate for cleared or closed homicide cases plummeted to roughly 30 percent, while suspected urban terrorists remained in the community. According to *The Baltimore Sun*:

"The closure rate is so low that detectives grouse that the year shouldn't even be counted. One likened it to baseball's steroid era, when players used performance-enhancing drugs to rewrite the record book. They say this year's homicide numbers should be marked with an asterisk: The Freddie Gray era."

Frighteningly, many of Baltimore's homicide victims were shot in broad daylight, oftentimes in the street, while others were collateral damage from urban terrorists' crossfire. Some fatalities occurred from bullets randomly fired into crowds, and almost two dozen victims were children, many of them toddlers. Yet, mum was the word. Even a year after three-year-old McKenzie Elliott was killed during a drive-by while playing on her porch, the case remains cold. *"Everyone was outside, so I know someone knows something,"* McKenzie's mother told WBAL. In the summer of 2014, McKenzie was among five victims — all black — murdered over the course of three days, and no one has been charged. At the time of the tragedy, a neighbor spoke to the local media and prophesized this present-day reality. He declared, *"No one's going to talk. No one's going to say anything and you can't blame them because once they do, their family is in jeopardy*[66]*. No one wants to lose their kids or their loved ones so no one's going to talk."* Investigators believe there are people in the neighborhood who know who's responsible but are refusing to come forward. If only little McKenzie's killers weren't black thugs, she would've qualified for BLM's benefits package and received national support. History has shown that combatting the "no-snitch" culture isn't a priority for BLM or RGI. That's why the NAACP had a mock funeral for the n-word, but never a mock funeral for the no-snitch mentality, or any other actual detriments to the black community.

Murder witness tells detectives victim 'wouldn't want me to say a thing'
baltimoresun.com

NAACP to hold funeral for 'N' word
usatoday.com

[Author's Note: Unsurprisingly, they held a symbolic funeral for the "N-Word" but not for the thugs who deliberately personify the "N-Word."]

McKenzie Elliott's Murderer Remains at Large, One Year Later
patch.com

McKenzie's family celebrated her fourth birthday at her grave site

The Unsung Hero

A black criminal subculture has a monopoly on inner-cities across America. The hood is its asylum to operate with impunity. As a gesture of appreciation, the criminals may perform acts of altruism such as, providing turkeys on Thanksgiving, sponsoring basketball tournaments, or even "making it rain" at local strip clubs. In the hood, this is how a criminal and community liability becomes a hero, while a true hero and community asset like Kendal Fenwick is treated like a hero sandwich.

Freddie Gray Empowerment Center opens
wtop.com

Empowering what? Criminality? Like its namesake?

Kendal Fenwick, a 24-year-old Baltimore father of three, was a martyr who died while fulfilling his natural responsibility: protecting his children. Not only was he protecting his kids, his courageous act was a preemptive strike against human cancer that plagues urban America.

In an attempt to prevent neighborhood drug dealers from going back and forth through the yard of his northwest Baltimore rowhome, Mr. Fenwick erected a fence. The move upset the drug dealers, but they continued to violate his space. Fed up, Mr. Fenwick confronted the dealers in front of his home. It cost him his life.

"He was cooking for the kids," recalled his children's mother. *"He told the children that it was firecrackers so they wouldn't... and my son heard them. They were in the closet. They heard him crying for help. That's the worst thing in the world."*

Setting aside any fear for his own life, police believe Fenwick's final act was to save the lives of those children.

"...when he was chased by these cowardly killers, he chose not to run back in his house because the three kids were in the house. So he ran around the side of the yard and they caught up with him and they executed him," said Police Commissioner Kevin Davis.

For all intents and purposes, Kendal Fenwick's story should be referenced for inspiration by hostages in every "hood," but since he shared the same pigmentation as human cancer that ultimately snatched his life, his death won't be deemed worthy of a recreation center or a center of any kind, including being the center of attention. An honorable man murdered in cold blood by dishonorable menaces, whose only connect to any type of honor is when they're addressing a judge in court, *"I dindu nuffin yo' honor."*

Police call murder victim Kendal Fenwick a 'model citizen'

abc2news.com

Didn't meet qualifications to have a rec center named in his honor

Chapter V

The Congressional Black Caucus

"If pigs could vote, the man with the slop bucket would be elected swineherd every time, no matter how much slaughtering he did on the side." - Orson Scott Card

The Congressional Black ~~Carcass~~ Caucus is the legislative arm of the RGI and represents roughly ten percent of the House of Representatives and about a fifth of the Democratic minority. Established in 1970, the Congressional Black Caucus (CBC) calls itself *"the Conscience of Congress."* Today, the "*Conscience of Congress"* does nothing more than beat victimology into Congress' head until Congress becomes unconscious.

Originally founded in 1969 as a "Democratic Select Committee" by a group of black members of the House of Representatives, the organization was renamed as the CBC in 1971. Although the CBC is officially non-partisan, it's a Democrat stronghold[67] — correction... black Democrat stronghold. When white liberal Congressman Steve Cohen pledged to his sixty-percent black district in Tennessee that he'd apply for CBC membership, the CBC made it crystal clear that membership entrance was based on pigmentation, not applications. While the bylaws of the caucus do not make race a prerequisite for membership, the consensus of the caucus is that it should remain exclusively black. Even though Representative Cohen introduced and championed House Resolution 194, which apologized for *"the enslavement and racial segregation of African-Americans[68],"* the CBC only saw color and not his commitment to people of color. *"Mr. Cohen asked for admission, and he got his answer. ... It's time to move on,"* said Rep. William Lacy Clay, Jr., D-MO., son of Rep. William Lacy Clay Sr., D-MO., a co-founder of the caucus. *"It's an unwritten rule. It's understood. It's clear."* Steve Cohen wasn't the first white Democrat denied membership. Politico.com reported that Rep. Pete Stark, D-Calif., tried in 1975 when he was a sophomore representative, and the group was only six years old.

"Half my Democratic constituents were African American. I felt we had interests in common as far as helping people in poverty," Stark said. *"They had a vote, and I lost. They said the issue was that I was white, and they felt it was important that the group be limited to African Americans."* For a group that touts itself as being passionate fighters for black interests, they're apparently more passionate about fighting for a separate existence.

Black Caucus: Whites Not Allowed
politico.com

#BlackVotesMatter

As the top-ranking black politicians in America, CBC members truly understand that #BlackVotesMatter. *"Black voters count, and they can make the difference. I want them to know that[69],"* said former CBC head, Rep. Emanuel Cleaver (D-MO.) — in reference to the CBC's "Voter-Protection" tour that featured free concerts for its voting bloc. The guaranteed method to secure the black vote is through black-identity politics. The black-identity politics — practiced by the CBC and many other black politicians — license them to campaign on the concept that black leadership will translate into black political power, and the acquired political power will be used to properly address black issues neglected under white leadership. Ultimately, black-identity politics perpetuate an *"us versus them"* mindset that compliments the victim mentality present amongst its constituency.

In Houston, black-identity politics even allowed a white conservative Republican — running in an overwhelmingly black Democrat district — to unseat a 24 year black incumbent on the Houston Community College Board of Trustees. The Houston Community College board is composed of nine members elected from single-member districts and serve six-year terms. Dave Wilson, a white small business owner who knew that winning the second district seat was a long-shot, told *KHOU.com* that he printed direct mail pieces that strongly implied he was black. His fliers were decorated with photographs of smiling African-American faces — which he readily admits he simply lifted off websites — and captioned with the words, *"Please vote for our friend and neighbor Dave Wilson."* The campaign was successful. Bruce Austin, the black incumbent who was unseated by assumed black man Dave Wilson, called Wilson's campaign deceitful. *"He never put out to voters that he was white," Austin said. "The problem is his picture was not in the League of Voters (pamphlet) or anywhere. This is one of the few times a white guy has pretended to be a black guy and fooled black people."*

White guy wins after leading voters to believe he's black
legacy.khou.com

Black-identity politics also prevent the CBC from criticizing President Obama. The appearance of racial solidarity trumps all racial dilemmas. Congresswoman Maxine Waters (D-CA.) once confessed as much to a Detroit crowd:

"We don't put pressure on the president, let me tell you why. We don't put pressure on the president because y'all love the president. You love the president. You're very proud...to have a black man [in the White House] ...First time in the history of the United States of America. If we go after the president too hard, you're going after us[70]."

Her colleague, Rep. Emanuel Cleaver (D-MO.), echoed her sentiment. While discussing the abysmal unemployment numbers in the black community with Root.com, Rep. Cleaver was asked if the black community gives President Obama a pass because he's black. Cleaver confirmed what anyone with at least one functioning eye could see.

"Look, as the chair of the Black Caucus I've got to tell you, we are always hesitant to criticize the president. With 14 percent [black] unemployment, if we had a white president we'd be marching around the White House[71]."

In the rare occurrence that voters break ranks and question the CBC's agenda, the CBC will step out of its bubble to place the sheep back into formation. Such was the case at a 2014 CBC town hall meeting; Rep. Marcia Fudge (D-OH.) chided the electorate for demanding more accountability from the CBC:

"I hope you will spend this much time with your local elected officials. I guarantee you most people in this room have not done that. With your school board, with your city council, and so then you won't be calling me talking about somebody didn't come and pick up your trash. You need to call your city council person for that. And I say it that way because, I need you to understand we all have a role to play and the Congressional Black Caucus cannot do it all by ourselves. Everybody has to do their part...The Black Caucus fights for you every day. Even when you won't fight for yourself. We fight for you. Whether it's immigration or education, whether it's food stamps or housing, we fight for you everyday. So my message to you is to contain your complaining[72]."

In other words, we fight to put foods stamps in your pocket and subsidized roofs over your heads, so shut up and keep blindly voting for us.

Because majority-black cities are more concerned with being bastions of black political power instead of models for economic growth and prosperity, they've instead become models of mayhem and dysfunction. At a 2002 NAACP conference, Philadelphia Mayor John Street, who would eventually serve two mayoral terms, boasted about the opportunities he'd given to blacks; how he'd hired a black police commissioner, a black fire commissioner, a black finance director, a black treasurer. *"The brothers and sisters are running the city,"* he proclaimed, *"Running it! Don't you let nobody fool you, we are in charge of the City of Brotherly Love[73]."* Among the ten largest cities, Philadelphia has the highest deep-poverty rate[74]. Walter E. Williams, an esteemed economist and George Mason University professor, addressed the pitfall of black-identity politics[75].

"Let's look at some of the strategy since the beginning of the civil rights movement. The black power movement of the '60s and '70s held that black underrepresentation in the political arena was a major problem. It was argued that the election of more black officials as congressmen, mayors and city council members would mean economic power, better neighborhoods and better schools. Forty-three years ago, there were roughly 1,500 black elected officials nationwide. According to the Joint Center for Political and Economic Studies, by 2011 there were roughly 10,500 black elected officials, including a black president. But what were the fruits?

By most any measure, the problems are worse. There is the greatest black poverty, poorest education, highest crime and greatest family instability in cities such as: Detroit, St. Louis, Oakland, Calif., Memphis, Tenn., Birmingham, Ala., Atlanta, Baltimore, Cleveland, Philadelphia and Buffalo, N.Y. The most common characteristic of these predominantly black cities is that, for decades, all of them have been run by Democratic and presumably liberal administrations. What's more is that in most of these cities, blacks have been mayors, chiefs of police, school superintendents and principals and have dominated city councils.

Political power has not lived up to its billing."

Ignoring Urban Terrorism

Part of the CBC's self-described goal is *"[p]ositively influencing the course of events pertinent to African-Americans[76]..."* If the CBC's goal of *"positively influencing the course of events pertinent to African-Americans"* were legitimate, then addressing the high crime rates in many of its members' heavily black areas would be the utmost priority. The CBC has 19 different task forces but none for the most pressing issue affecting black communities: urban terrorism.

- Africa Taskforce
- Budget, Appropriations, and Taxation Taskforce
- Civil Rights and Judiciary Taskforce
- Diversity Taskforce
- Economic Development and Wealth Creation Taskforce
- Education and Labor Taskforce
- Education Reform Working Group
- Energy, Environment, and Agriculture Taskforce
- Foreign Affairs and National Security Taskforce
- Healthcare Reform Implementation Working Group
- Healthcare Taskforce
- Immigration Reform Taskforce
- Judicial Nominations Working Group
- Justice System Reform Working Group
- Poverty and the Economy Taskforce
- Prison Telecomm Reform Working Group
- Technology and Infrastructure Development
- Voter Protection and Empowerment Working Group

Like clockwork, urban terrorism has ensured that black cities typically possess the highest crime rates in America compared to other communities of all sizes - from the smallest towns to the largest cities. Yet, even with statistical evidence, most black legislators lack the fortitude and/or desire to address this unflattering reality. Many cities within the CBC members' districts are quintessential representations of black urban dysfunction and mainstays on the disgraceful list of America's most dangerous cities. Honestly, the CBC's apathy isn't surprising. After all, black thugs aren't criticized for the same reason President Obama isn't criticized: black-identity politics. Skin folk is kinfolk... except black conservatives. Furthermore, there's no political capital to be gained from addressing black intraracial genocide — unless Willie Lynch, racism, Post Traumatic Slavery Disorder (PTSD), or guns can be blamed. As a result, many of their districts will remain awash with urban terrorism and designated as "no-go" zones. In 2015, Milwaukee, Baltimore, Washington, D.C., New Orleans, and Kansas City saw their murder rate increase double-digits.

Black Lives Matter Would Like To See A Little More Help From Congressional Black Caucus
huffingtonpost.com

Cleveland & Columbus, OH

Representative Marcia L. Fudge's Eleventh Congressional District is 54 percent black and includes majority black populated Cleveland (53 percent), which Forbes magazine listed as America's eighth most dangerous city in 2015 —populations above 200,000. Cleveland ranked twenty-third on *NeighborhoodScout.com's* list of *America's Most Dangerous Cities* — populations over 25,000. With its crime index ranking of two out of 100 (100 being the safest), Cleveland is only safer than two-percent of American cities. And within Ohio, more than 99 percent of the communities have a lower crime rate than Cleveland. One's chances of becoming a victim of either violent or property crime are one in fifteen. Four of the *Top 100 Worst Performing Public Schools in the U.S.[77]* are in Cleveland, including one named after George Washington Carver.

Experts struggle to explain rise in Cleveland gun violence
bigstory.ap.org

During the first nine months of 2015, Cleveland saw a 40 percent increase in homicides and a 33 percent rise in felonious assault shootings (compared to the same period in 2014). Five children under the age of 17 were shot over the Fourth of July holiday weekend, and a four-week span in autumn produced three children, whose combined ages only equaled eight and a half years, shot and killed from drive-by shootings. A witness to the murder of three-year-old Major Howard told *Newnet5.com* that gunshots were *"normal"* in his neighborhood. *"It's Cleveland,"* he elaborated, *"You're going to hear a lot of gunshots ... but to see a little boy get hit or a female get hit, that's just different."*

Witness to 3-year-old's murder calls gunshots 'normal
newsnet5.com

5-month-old Aavielle, 3-year-old Major, and 5-year-old Ramon Burnett

So, what is Rep. Fudge's strategy to counter the harsh violence that occurs year after year in her district? Well, she decided to use her floor speech at the House of Representatives to disparage the police shootings of black males, and cite the shootings as symptoms of America's pervasive racism. *"The fact that our country, the greatest country in the world, remains mired in race relations issues in the year 2014 is an embarrassment,"* decried Fudge.

5 children shot in Cleveland over Fourth of July weekend; at least 11 total people shot
newsnet5.com

Rep. Marcia Fudge decries Ferguson and Cleveland police shootings in Black Caucus floor speech
cleveland.com

Rep. Marcia L. Fudge (D)

Representative Joyce Beatty's Third Congressional District is 32 percent black and includes most of 28 percent black Columbus, which faces the same bloody issues as its larger Cleveland sibling. In Columbus, one's chances of becoming a victim of either violent or property crime there are one in twenty, and with a crime index ranking of seven out of a 100 (100 being the safest), Columbus is only safer than seven percent of American cities. Within Ohio, more than 95 percent of the communities have a lower crime rate than Columbus.

16-Year-Old Suspect Arrested In North Columbus Quadruple Homicide
10tv.com

Quadruple homicide victims: Michael Ballour, 41, Daniel Sharp 36, Angela Harrison, 35, Tyajah Nelson, 18

Columbus' 2016 began with five homicides in its first week. In 2015, blacks accounted for most of Columbus' homicide victims and perpetrators. And two of Columbus' 20 police precincts bore the brunt of 2015's 99 homicides[78]. Approximately 30 percent of the city's homicides occurred in precincts that make up only 7 percent of its population. Columbus' police department is concerned about the city's climbing murder rate, especially among those under 30 years old. In 2014, black males overwhelmingly made up the largest group of the town's 89 homicides — many of the victims were under 30 years old. The trend hasn't changed.

Columbus Police Grow Concerned As Murder Rate Climbs Among Those Under 30
10tv.com

Deadly start to 2016 in Columbus; 5 homicides in first week
nbc4i.com

So, who's responsible for black lives not mattering in Cleveland and Columbus? The answer won't shock Reps. Fudge and Beatty; they already know that it's not "racist cops," but black males. However, their Hypocritical Oath and black-identity politics prevent honesty.

Rep. Joyce Beatty (D)

St. Louis & Kansas City, MO

Representative William Lacy Clay's First Congressional District includes the majority-black city of St. Louis (49 percent), which Forbes magazine recognized as America's fourth most dangerous city in 2015 with populations over 200,000. *NeighborhoodScout.com* ranked St. Louis third on its 2016 list of Top 30 U.S. Cities with the highest murder rate — 25,000 or more people, and twelfth on its 2016 list of *100 Most Dangerous cities in America* — with 25,000 or more people. Moreover, its crime index ranking is one out of 100 (100 is the safest), meaning St. Louis is safer than only one percent of American cities. One's chances of becoming a victim of either violent or property crime there are one in 12. Within Missouri, more than 98 percent of the communities have a lower crime rate than St. Louis.

St. Louis' 2014 concluded with 159 homicides — leaving the city with a murder rate of 50 per 100,000 residents, the worst in the nation for larger cities. Ninety-five percent of defendants in 2014 were black and 91 percent were male — 55 percent were 25 and under. Furthermore, from January 2014 through August 2015, 90 percent of murder victims were black. Eighty-five percent were male, and 48 percent were aged 25 and under. Its 2015 homicide count was 188; a significant increase for a city that already had a high homicide rate a year prior.

2015 Was St. Louis' Deadliest Year in Two Decades
riverfronttimes.com

A *Riverfront Times* analysis[79] of police data revealed a familiar pattern to inner-city police: the homicides are clustered. Since 2008, about 80 percent of homicides have occurred in just a third of St. Louis' neighborhoods. Richard Rosenfeld, a criminologist at the University of Missouri-St. Louis who regularly consults with city police was surprised when he crunched the numbers from 2000 through 2014 according to the article. He found that half of St. Louis' violent crime was concentrated on just five percent of city blocks. My bet is that one of those blocks included N. Newstead Avenue/Cote Brilliante Avenue, which *NeighborhoodScout.com* listed as the fourteenth most dangerous American neighborhood in 2015.

ST. LOUIS: 6-YEAR-OLD HEART PATIENT KILLED IN DRIVE-BY SHOOTING AT O'FALLEN PARK
inquisitr.com

6-year-old Marcus Johnson Jr. was shot and killed over a "traffic dispute." A week earlier, he underwent heart surgery and had a post-operation check-up scheduled on his fatal day.

A St. Louis police officer posted a vivid account of his encounter with critically wounded Marcus Johnson Jr. at Children's Hospital. The sympathetic officer wrote[80] (via "Don of all Trades" blog):

We arrived at the Children's Hospital Emergency Room at the same time. He and his partner parked and I pulled up to their left and did the same. I got out of my car and watched as the officer hurried from his seat and opened the back, driver's side door. When the officer grabbed the boy from the back seat of his police Tahoe, I knew almost instantly. There was a split second though, before instantly I guess, where I didn't know. For that split second, the officer looked like any dad grabbing his sleeping boy from the car and putting the boy's head on his shoulder to carry him inside to sleep comfortably in his own bed. For that split second, it was a sweet moment. The officer, an around fifty year old white guy, clutched the little boy over his left shoulder gently, but with a clear purpose. The boy was small, a black child with his hair in corn rows and dressed as a typical five or six-year-old dresses. He reminded me of my own six-year-old son. The sudden, pained look on the officer's face and the fact that the boy wasn't crying or yelling or doing anything other than appearing to be asleep made the split second fantasy fade away fast. We hurried into the emergency room where we were met by the trauma team and hospital staff. I'm always in awe at how these emergency room doctors and nurses and staff are so able to get to working on a patient so fast. There was some sliver of hope that the boy would make it, at least that's what we all wanted to believe. The truth, and I think we all knew it, was that this boy would never fall asleep in his own bed again. When the officer laid the boy down on the gurney and stood back upright, any wind that may have been in my sails quickly faded to nothing. His shirt said it all. Where the boy's little heart had laid so close to the officer's own heart, was a mess that told us things would not end well.

The officer who carried 6-year-old Marcus. Cops > Politicians

So, what is Congressman's Clay's strategy to counter the unforgiving violence that occurs year after year in his district? Well, marching for Mike Brown should suffice. Right?

Rep. Clay posted this picture on his website with the caption, *"Marching for justice for Michael Brown and his family in Ferguson. MO"*

Rep. Wm. Lacy Clay (D)

Representative Emanuel Cleaver's Fifth Congressional District encompasses Kansas City, which is 29.9 percent black. *NeighborhoodScout.com* ranked Kansas City thirty-fourth on its

2016 list of *100 Most Dangerous Cities in America* — with 25,000 or more people. Moreover, its crime index ranking is four out of 100 (100 being the safest), meaning Kansas City is only safer than four percent of American cities. One's chances of becoming a victim of either violent or property crime there are one in 16. Within Missouri, more than 94 percent of the communities have a lower crime rate than Kansas City. Additionally, K.C. has the twenty-third most dangerous neighborhood in America — Brush Creek Blvd./Prospect Ave. — according to *NeighborhoodScout.com's* list of *Top 25 Most Dangerous Neighborhoods in America.*

Kansas City man kills 2 teens then allegedly shoots his baby for crying
kctv5.com

The victims: Bianca Fletcher, 1-year-old Joseph, Shannon Rollins Jr.

In 2015, Kansas City experienced 109 homicides, making it one of the deadliest years in recent history. According to *Kansascity.com*, September was a particularly bad month with twenty deaths, including the shooting deaths of a south Kansas City teenage mother, her one-year-old son, and 18-year-old boyfriend. The final number of homicides in September was one short of the city's most deadly month when 21 people were killed in August 2008. Young people between the ages of 17 and 24 were the most prevalent victims, constituting 40 percent of those killed and unsurprisingly, black males constituted the largest number of homicide victims: 63 percent. In October 2015, police reported that at least 16 children were murdered since the previous October. Shootings killed many of the children, who ranged from six weeks to 16 years old, in their homes, on their neighborhood streets, or walking beside their parents. Ten-year-old Machole "Coco" Stewart was shot in the head while watching the World Series with her family after a gunman sprayed 20 bullets into the house. Following the tragedy, her grandmother expressed to KCTV the need for more outrage about black-on-black violence. (Eureka moment indeed!)

"They are killing our kids and nobody cares about it. It's just vigils, balloons let go. Why not get out here and rally? We are having black-on-black crime killing each other but then when a Caucasian kills an African-American everybody wants to go rally, everybody wants to go march. Why not rally, why not march while they are killing our kids."

A local pastor urged those with information to speak to the authorities.

"Those who know what happened, those who were involved, I know some of you are in the room right now. You know who it is. You know who done it."

Machole Stewart's murder is still unsolved.

Slain girl's grandmother: Where is outrage?
kctv.com

1 year later, Machole Stewart's family still searching for answers as police search for killer
fox10tv.com

2015 was Kansas City's deadliest year for homicides since 2011
kansascity.com

Coco Stewart loved school and dancing

So, who's responsible for black lives not mattering in St. Louis and Kansas City? The answer won't shock Reps. Clay and Cleaver; they already know that it's black males, not Darren "The Gentle Giant Slayer" Wilson, and his co-conspirators. Nonetheless, the Congressmen's allegiance to the Hypocritical Oath and black-identity politics prevent honesty.

Rep. Emanuel Cleaver (D)

Detroit, MI

There are two hells in Michigan. One is a tourist attraction (Hell, Michigan) and the other is Detroit. Flint, with its 71 percent increase in homicides from 2014 to 2015, receives an honorable mention[81]. The 13th and 14th Congressional Districts have been redistricted but still, include much of Detroit (83 percent black). These districts are represented by John Conyers Jr. and Brenda Lawrence respectively. Expectedly, for the third consecutive year, Forbes magazine recognized Detroit as America's most dangerous city (in cities with populations over 200,000). *NeighborhoodScout.com* ranked Detroit fifth on its 2016 list of *Top 30 U.S. Cities with the Highest Murder Rates* — 25,000 or more people — and third on its 2016 list of *100 Most Dangerous Cities in America.* Moreover, its crime index ranking is two out of 100 (100 is the safest), meaning Detroit is only safer than two percent of American cities. One's chances of becoming a victim of either violent or property crime there are one in 15. Within Michigan, more than 99 percent of the communities have a lower crime rate than Detroit. The "Motor City" is also home to the tenth (W Warren Ave. / McKinley St.) and sixteenth (Trumbull St./Lincoln St.) most dangerous U.S. neighborhoods — according to *NeighborhoodScout.com's Top 25 Most Dangerous Neighborhoods in America.* One's chances of becoming victimized in those areas are one in 13 and one in 14, respectively.

America's Most Dangerous Cities: Detroit Can't Shake No. 1 Spot
forbes.com

Although seven people were killed over the 2015 Labor Day weekend, Detroit's 295 homicides in 2015 were actually an improvement from the 299 homicides in 2014 — the year its police chief called upon law-abiding citizens to arm themselves against criminals. The ninth police precinct, located on Detroit's east side, recorded 46 homicides, the most of any precinct[82].

7-year-old killed, 8-year-old wounded in Steel Street shooting
fox2detroit.com

An argument between two baby mamas over their shared baby daddy lead to 7-year-old Chanel Berry being killed when her house was sprayed with bullets.

So, who's responsible for black lives not mattering in Detroit? Detroit Police Chief James Craig knows the answer. In fact, after 47 gunshots were fired at a crowd of 400 people gathered at a Detroit basketball court (injuring 11 and killing one spectator); he accurately called them out as *"urban terrorists."* Reps. Fudge and Beatty already know it's the "urban terrorists," but their Hypocritical Oath and black-identity politics prevent honesty.

Detroit Police Chief James Craig defends 'urban terrorist' comment
mlive.com

Reps. Brenda Lawrence (D) & John Conyers, Jr. (D)

Newark and Trenton, NJ

Representative Donald M. Payne, Jr.'s 10th Congressional District includes majority-black Newark (52 percent), also called "Brick City" because of its numerous brick housing projects. Newark is New Jersey's largest city, and was once known as the "*car theft capital of the world.*" It has long been one of the state's most dangerous cities and ranked fourteenth on *NeighborhoodScout.com's* 2016 list of *Top 30 U.S. Cities with the Highest Murder Rates* — 25,000 or more people — and fifty-first on its 2016 list of *100 Most Dangerous Cities in America.* Moreover, its crime index ranking is 11 out of 100 (100 is the safest), meaning Newark is only safer than 11 percent of American cities. One's chances of becoming a victim of either violent or property crime there are one in 24. Relative to New Jersey, Newark has a crime rate that is higher than 95 percent of the state's cities and towns of all sizes. "Brick City" is also home to the eleventh most dangerous U.S. neighborhood — Lincoln St./Court St. — according to *NeighborhoodScout.com's Top 25 Most Dangerous Neighborhoods in America.* One's chances of becoming victimized in that area are one in 13.

Newark Boy, 3, Is Fatally Struck by Suspect's Car in Police Chase
nytimes.com

[Article's Quote: "This area is very prone to car stealings, carjackings. It's real bad, real bad, this area," said Rahmere's grandmother.]

3-year-old Rahmere Tullus died carrying his new Spider-Man book bag

In 2015, Newark saw a surge in violence, including five killings over two days in August. Those slayings prompted city officials to take 115 police officers off desk duty and send them out to patrol the city's streets.

Homicides and Shootings Both Up in Newark in 2015
wsj.com

So, who's responsible for black lives not mattering in Newark? The answer won't shock Rep. Payne; he already knows that it's not "racist cops," but black males. However, the Hypocritical Oath and black-identity politics prevent honesty.

Rep. Donald M. Payne, Jr. (D)

Not to be outdone by its bigger sibling, New Jersey's capital city of Trenton (52 percent black), which falls into Representative Bonnie Watson Coleman's Twelfth Congressional District, ranked ninth on NeighborhoodScout's 2016 list of *Top 30 American Cities with the Highest Murder Rate* — 25,000 or more people. Additionally, Trenton placed forty-ninth on its 2016 list of *100 Most Dangerous Cities in America*. Moreover, its crime index ranking is fifteenth out of 100 (100 is the safest), which means that it's only safer than 15 percent of American cities. The chances of becoming a victim of either violent or property crime in Trenton are one in 28. Relative to New Jersey, Trenton has a crime rate that is higher than 91 percent of the state's cities and towns of all sizes. In 2015, Trenton's murder rate was more than twice that of major U.S. cities such as Philadelphia and Chicago[83]. Also, its practice of urban omerta remained consistent with other larger and smaller inner cities. Trenton's East Ward Councilwoman, Verlina Reynolds-Jackson, acknowledged the self-inflicted crisis[84]: *"[t]his attitude of not snitching is really what's hurting us. People know who commits these crimes, and we have a plethora of ways for citizens to provide anonymous tips. The best thing we can do is report the violence."*

Teenager murdered in Trenton Friday night
trenton.homicidewatch.org

16-year-old Jah'vae Minney's 2015 death was Trenton's third murder within a week

So, who's responsible for black lives not mattering in Trenton? The answer won't shock Rep. Watson; she already knows that it's not "racist cops," but black males. However, the Hypocritical Oath and black-identity politics prevent honesty.

Rep. Bonnie Watson Coleman (D)

Chicago, IL

Representative Bobby L. Rush's First Congressional District includes much of the South Side of Chicago and once had the highest percentage of African-American residents of any Congressional District in the nation until it was redistricted in 2013. Presently, the district maintains a 51.3 percent black majority. Representative Robin Kelly's Second Congressional District is predominantly black (55.5 percent), and includes sections of Chicago. Representative Danny K. Davis' Seventh Congressional District also has a black majority (54.6 percent) and includes parts of Chicago. Interestingly, blacks make up only a quarter of Chicago's populace, yet these three CBC member's districts are majority-black. Even so, Chicago consistently has enough murder to cover all their districts.

The nation's third largest city recorded 51 homicides in January 2016, the highest toll for the month since at least 2000, and 241 shooting incidents — more than double the 119 incidents recorded in January 2015. By 2015's end, the 468 homicides were a 12.5 percent increase and 2,900 shootings jumped 13 percent than the prior year. *NeighborhoodScout.com* reports that the chances of becoming a victim of either violent or property crime in Chicago are one in 25. Relative to Illinois, Chicago has a crime rate that is higher than 94 percent of the state's cities and towns of all sizes. Furthermore, it possesses the twenty-fourth most dangerous American neighborhood — S. Pulaski Rd./W. Adams St. — as listed on *NeighborhoodScout.com's Top 25 Most Dangerous Neighborhoods in America*. One's chances of being victimized in that area are one in 17. In this diverse city where blacks, whites, and Latinos each roughly represent a third of the population, only one group consistently represents the "die" in diversity.

Police: "Significant" increase in Chicago murders, shootings in 2015
cbsnews.com

So, who's responsible for black lives not mattering in Chicago? The answer won't shock Reps. Rush, Davis, and Kelly; they already know that it's not the "racist police" but black males. Nonetheless, the Hypocritical Oath and black-identity politics prevent honesty. Actually, Rep. Kelly has already answered the question about the cause of violence in her 2014 report. And naturally, she blames guns and not violent people with guns. In her 2014 report[85], *"Gun Violence in America,"* she focused on blacks who died by guns and noted that blacks accounted for fifty-five percent of the national gun murder victims. *"If New Orleans were a country, it would be the second deadliest nation in the world, with a gun murder rate of 62.1 per 100,000 citizens. Detroit's murder rate mirrors El Salvador,"* the report said. *"Chicago is a carbon copy of Guyana. Washington, D.C., our nation's capital, has a higher gun homicide rate than Brazil — a nation that has long experienced high crime rates stemming from narcotics trafficking and other violent gang activity."* Calling it gun violence is as asinine as calling it bullet violence.

Reps. Bobby Rush (D) Danny Davis (D) Robin Kelly (D)

Milwaukee, WI

Representative Gwen Moore's Fourth Congressional District encompasses the majority black city of Milwaukee (40 percent). For several years, Milwaukee ranked among the ten most dangerous large cities in the United States. In fact, Forbes magazine recognized Milwaukee as America's sixth most dangerous city in 2015 — with populations over 200,000. *NeighborhoodScout.com* ranked Milwaukee fifteenth on its 2016 list of *100 Most Dangerous Cities in America* — with 25,000 or more people. Moreover, its crime index ranking is three out of 100 (100 being the safest), which means it's only safer than three percent of American cities. One's chances of becoming a victim of either violent or property crime there are one in 16. Within Wisconsin, more than 98 percent of the communities have a lower crime rate than Milwaukee. Furthermore, it possesses the eighteenth most dangerous American neighborhood — W. Clybourn St. / N. 27th St. — as listed on *NeighborhoodScout.com's Top 25 Most Dangerous Neighborhoods in America.* One's chances of being victimized in that area are one in 14.

Teen remembered in vigil as wave of violence hits Milwaukee

jsonline.com

A Facebook dispute over a girl led to the shooting death of 14yo Tariq Akbar by a 15yo boy

In 2015, Milwaukee recorded 145 homicides, not including six fatal shootings that were ruled self-defense, or the death of a man who suffered heart failure after a robbery. According to the Journal Sentinel, Milwaukee's 2015 homicide tally was almost a 69 percent increase from 2014. Additionally, this year-to-year growth was higher than the headline-grabbing spikes of violence reported in Baltimore, St. Louis, and Washington, D.C. Milwaukee's Police Chief, Edward Flynn, cited a few factors for the city's mounting homicide toll including a subculture within the city that affirms the use of deadly violence to achieve status. In parts of Milwaukee, the sound of gunfire is so commonplace that about 80 percent of gunshots detected by ShotSpotter sensors — an expensive technology system designed to detect and pinpoint gunfire leading to quicker police response — aren't even called into police by residents, Flynn said.

Latest homicides push Milwaukee total to highest in a decade
jsonline.com

Homicides soar in Milwaukee, along with many theories on cause
jsonline.com

In 2014, Chief Flynn became a notable, national figure when he ranted (in part):

"The greatest racial disparity in the city of Milwaukee is getting shot and killed. Hello! Eighty percent of my homicide victims every year are African-American. Eighty percent of our aggravated assault victims are African-American. Eighty percent of our shooting victims, who survive their shooting, are African-American...."

The rant was in response to armchair activists attacking the police chief and department for a white officer killing a black male while ignoring the killing of a five-year-old girl shot in a drive-by while sitting indoors on her grandfather's lap. Two months later, thirteen-month-old "Baby Bill" Thao was shot and killed while playing with Legos on a floor. Darmequaye Cohill, a drug-dealing urban terrorist, whose first name characteristically reads like a handful of random letters grabbed from a Scrabble pouch, fired forty-one shots at the wrong house in a dispute with another drug-dealing urban terrorist. Even so, the armchair activists' vitriol remains reserved for Milwaukee's Finest.

Milwaukee Police Chief Flynn's take on crime, racial disparities goes viral
jsonline.com

In 2016, nine-year-old Za'layia Jenkins approached officers on foot patrol in her neighborhood and asked why were they there. The officers replied that they walked the neighborhood to help keep it safe. The inquisitive nine-year-old then asked if they could keep her safe. Approximately a week later, little Za'layia was shot while watching television when a bullet from a shootout between urban terrorists pierced a wall of her home. More than forty shell casings were recovered from the crime scene. *"Sadly, that question was answered tonight,"* Chief Flynn said after "Lay-Lay" (as she was affectionately called) was shot. Tragically, this innocent girl — who also jumped rope with one of the officers a week earlier — died from her head wound a day before her tenth birthday.

9-year-old girl who was struck by errant bullet in home dies

jsonline.com

Lay-Lay's family said she was energetic and always smiled

So, who's responsible for black lives not mattering in Milwaukee? The answer won't shock Rep. Moore; she already knows that it's not "racist cops," but black males. Nonetheless, the Hypocritical Oath and black-identity politics prevent honesty.

Rep. Gwen Moore (D)

New Orleans & Baton Rouge, LA

Representative Cedric Richmond's Second Congressional District contains nearly all of the majority-black city of New Orleans (60 percent) and stretches west and north to the majority-black city of Baton Rouge (54 percent). The Baton Rouge area was picked up because of redistricting in 2010. *NeighborhoodScout.com* ranked New Orleans seventh on its 2016 list of *Top 30 U.S. Cities with the Highest Murder Rates* — 25,000 or more people, and twelfth on its 2016 list of *100 Most Dangerous Cities in America*. Moreover, its crime index ranking is five out of 100 (100 is the safest), which means it's only safer than five percent of American cities. One's chances of becoming a victim of either violent or property crime there are one in 19. Relative to Louisiana, New Orleans has a crime rate that is higher than 86 percent of the state's cities and towns of all sizes.

New Orleans violence claims men, women, children -- even babies in utero: Jarvis DeBerry
nola.com

Days before due date, parents were killed when urban terrorists shot up car

New Orleans, a city of about 380,000, also known as the "Big Easy" easily maintains a per-capita murder rate that's one of the highest in the country. Since 2010, almost 1,000 people have been murdered there[86]. Its 2015 homicide count eclipsed that of 2014 and included a deadly stretch of seven murders within an eight-day span. The city's festive vibe is constantly threatened by a far-reaching vibe of violence. In fact, Leon Cannizzaro, Orleans Parish District Attorney determined that the city was being dominated by "urban terrorists," and implored Governor Bobby Jindal to deploy state troopers. Evidently, the New Orleans Police

Department — like many other police departments — isn't equipped to handle urban terrorism.

2015 homicide total exceeds last year's after eastern New Orleans double shooting

Orleans DA blasts Jindal, says 'urban terrorists' in his own backyard

Baton Rouge has also secured a spot on *NeighborhoodScout's* Top 30 American Cities with the highest murder rate — 25,000 or more people. It is number twenty-nine, and one's chances of becoming a victim of either violent or property crime there are one in 18. Within Louisiana, more than 89 percent of the communities have a lower crime rate than Baton Rouge. Moreover, its crime index ranking is five out of 100 (100 is the safest), which means it's only safer than five percent of American cities. Fifty percent of 2015's homicide victims were black males age 15 to 35. The police clearance rate for the Baton Rouge police department was an abysmal 45 percent.

Pregnant woman shot, killed in Baton Rouge; unborn child delivered at hospital

Brittney Mills was shot and killed in her home. Her unborn baby died a week later

So, who's responsible for black lives not mattering in New Orleans and Baton Rouge? The answer won't shock Rep. Richmond; he already knows that it's not "racist cops," but black males. Nonetheless, the Hypocritical Oath and black-identity politics prevent honesty.

Baton Rouge homicides rise in 2015, an uptick after two years of decline

Rep. Cedric Richmond (D)

Indianapolis, IN

Representative André Carson's Seventh Congressional District encompasses Indianapolis, which was 2015's tenth most dangerous city with a populace over 200,000 according to Forbes.com. Its 2015 murder rate for every 100,000 residents was even higher than Chicago's murder rate for every 100,000 residents. Thus, *NeighborhoodScout.com* ranked Indianapolis eleventh on its 2016 list of *100 Most Dangerous Cities in America* — with 25,000 or more people. Moreover, Indy's 2015 crime index ranking was three out of 100 (100 being the safest), which means that it's considered safer than only three percent of American cities. One's chances of becoming a victim of either violent or property crime there are one in 16. Relative to Indiana, Indianapolis has a crime rate that is higher than 99 percent of the state's cities and towns of all sizes.

'It's like a war zone': Indy records its deadliest year in 2015
indystar.com

As reported by the Indy Star:

A homicide the night of Sept. 19 broke the hearts of nearly all who heard the tale.

That was the night 10-year-old Deshaun Swanson was fatally shot while attending a memorial service with his mother and 11-year-old brother.

The family was paying their final respects to an elderly woman when shots rang out. Three other people were hurt in the shooting, and Swanson died later that night in the hospital.

Less than a year after his death, residents of this crime-plagued neighborhood held a safety and rally march to celebrate 200 days without a homicide. In actuality, the murder-free

---

milestone was more of a testament than achievement. Even so, I applaud the hostages for finally fighting their captors.

10-year-old DeShaun Swanson

Safety rally and march to mark 200 days without a homicide in Butler Tarkington neighborhood
fox59.com

So, who's responsible for black lives not mattering in Indianapolis? The answer won't shock Rep. Carson; he already knows that it's not "racist cops," but black males. Nonetheless, the Hypocritical Oath and black-identity politics prevent honesty.

Rep. André Carson (D)

Jackson, MS

Representative Bennie Thompson's Second Congressional District is the only majority-black district in the state and includes most of the super-majority black (79 percent) city of Jackson. Of Mississippi's 10 largest cities, only seven report their crime statistics to the FBI for the twice-yearly Uniform Crime Report. Jackson, the state's capital, and largest city, reports their crime stats each year. Jackson ranked eleventh on *NeighborhoodScout.com's* 2016 list of *Top 30 American Cities with the Highest Murder Rate* — 25,000 or more people, and seventy-sixth on its 2016 list of *100 Most Dangerous Cities in America*. Moreover, its crime index ranking is two out of 100 (100 being the safest), which means that Jackson is considered safer than only two percent of U.S. cities. One's chances of becoming a victim of either violent or property crime there are one in 14. Relative to Mississippi, Jackson has a crime rate that is higher than 98 percent of the state's cities and towns of all sizes.

FOX 40 Investigates: How dangerous Is Jackson?
msnewsnow.com

[Article's Quote: "[T]he Capital City also had the fourth-highest murder rate in the country, when using the same criteria."

So, who's responsible for black lives not mattering in Jackson? The answer won't shock Rep. Thompson; he already knows that it's not "racist cops," but black males. Nonetheless, the Hypocritical Oath and black-identity politics prevent honesty.

Rep. Bennie Thompson (D)

Birmingham, AL

Representative Terri A. Sewell's Seventh Congressional District encompasses super-majority black (73 percent) Birmingham. Forbes lists Birmingham as the fifth most dangerous American city in 2015 — with populations over 200,000. NeighborhoodScout.com ranked Birmingham twenty-fifth on its 2015 list of Top 30 U.S. Cities with the Highest Murder Rates — 25,000 or more people, and twelfth on its 2016 list of 100 Most Dangerous Cities in America. Moreover, Birmingham's crime index ranking is one out of 100 (100 being the safest), which means it is considered safer than only one percent of American cities. One's chances of becoming a victim of either violent or property crime there are one in 12. Relative to Alabama, Birmingham has a crime rate that is higher than 98 percent of the state's cities and towns of all sizes. Birmingham's 2015 homicide count increased 55 percent from 2014, making 2015 the city's deadliest year since 2008.

Birmingham, Jefferson County end 2015 with dramatic rise in homicides
al.com

Frustrated with Birmingham's violence and the black clergy's apathy, Reverend Michael Jordan vented to *AL.com*:

"Our young black men are dying. I think it gets too much attention when a white policeman kills a black male, but it gets no attention when it's black on black murders."

Birmingham pastor's public prayer: 'Lord, please stop blacks from killing blacks'
al.com

Consequently, the concerned reverend attempted to rally black pastors and leaders by posting stark messages on his church's marquee. One side of the marquee read, *"Lord Please Stop Blacks From Killing Blacks,"* while the flip side read, *"Young Black Males Must Respect Authority."*

Mission impossible: Rev. Jordan stated that he didn't receive one call from black pastors or leaders

So, who's responsible for black lives not mattering in Birmingham? The answer won't shock Rep. Sewell; she already knows that it's not the ghost of Bull Connor or "racist cops," but black males. Nonetheless, the Hypocritical Oath and black-identity politics prevent honesty.

Rep. Terri A. Sewell (D)

Philadelphia, PA

Representative Chaka Fattah's Second Congressional District, which he has represented since 1995, includes much of majority-black (43 percent) Philadelphia. Affectionately called the "City of Brotherly Love," the brotherly love nowadays is the kind of love that Cain showed Abel. Philadelphia was once the murder capital of America and earned the moniker "Killadelphia." Presently, one's chances of becoming a victim of either violent or property crime there are one in 23. Relative to Pennsylvania, Philadelphia has a crime rate that is higher than 95 percent of the state's cities and towns of all sizes. Moreover, its crime index ranking is ten out of 100 (100 is the safest), which means it's considered safer than only 10 percent of American cities. Furthermore, it possesses the twenty-fifth most dangerous American neighborhood — N. 15th St./W. Dauphin St. — as listed on *NeighborhoodScout.com's Top 25 Most Dangerous Neighborhoods in America.* One's chances of being victimized in that area are one in 17. In this city, where one's zip code can predict one's life expectancy, 11-year-old Christian O'Hara expressed to philly.com that he thinks endlessly about bullets:

The 11-year-old says that when he hears gunshots in Fairhill, North Philadelphia, he feels painful pressure in his belly. "And," the soulful, dark-haired boy adds, "I know if a bullet hits me, it will feel worse than my stomach does." I feel stressed and scared, always. It needs to stop."

In Philly your zip code sets your life expectancy
philly.com

Only half of Philadelphia's 2015 homicides (52 percent) were solved — national average is 64 percent — despite the city's $20,000 reward for anyone who offers information leading to the arrest and conviction of a killer. Police cite the persistent "stop snitching" culture as an undeniable factor for its low homicide clearance rate. Ten of the *Top 100 Worst Performing Public Schools in the U.S.*[87] are in Philadelphia, including Martin Luther King High (Oh, the irony), Philadelphia Learning Academy (Learning what?), and John Bartram High, a school where daily assaults on staff caused a principal to quit.

PHILADELPHIA VIOLENT CRIME RATE ON THE RISE
6abc.com

With half of 2015's murders unsolved, effect of Philly cash rewards is questioned
newsworks.org

The Germantown section of Philadelphia, founded by German Quakers and Mennonites in 1683, has some of the country's best-maintained historic landmarks, districts, cobblestone streets, and buildings from the colonial era. Many of these structures, including the home where George Washington stayed to escape Yellow Fever, remain open to the public. Germantown is also the birthplace of America's anti-slavery movement and home to the first bank of the United States.

But what does all this wonderful Germantown history mean to the average Germantown citizen? Nothing. Today's Germantown is a shadow of its former self and has a victimization rate that rivals small cities. It desperately needs the German Quakers and Mennonites to return.

History remembers that on October 4, 1777, the colonials attacked British units that were housed in Germantown and *"The Battle of Germantown"* ensued. Understandably, history won't remember the modern day battle that's occurring in Germantown because it's not against the Redcoats... it's against the hoodies.

The present-day colonials should yell, *"The hoodies are coming...the hoodies are coming!"*

So, who's responsible for black lives not mattering in Philly? The answer won't shock Rep. Fattah; he already knows that it's not "racist cops," but black males. Nonetheless, the Hypocritical Oath and black-identity politics prevent honesty. However, this career politician is presently focused on his own troubles over those related to his constituency. He's currently facing a 29-count indictment for participation in a racketeering conspiracy and other crimes, including bribery; conspiracy to commit mail, wire, and honest services fraud; and multiple counts of mail fraud, falsification of records, bank fraud, making false statements to a financial institution, and money laundering. His son, Chaka Fattah Jr. — known as "Chip" — was recently found guilty on 22 of 23 counts of tax and bank fraud and sentenced to five years in prison. Did the apple fall far from the tree?

Congressman Chaka Fattah and Associates Charged with Participating in Racketeering Conspiracy
justice.gov

Chaka Fattah Jr. Sentenced to Five Years, Taken Into Custody
phillymag.com

[Author's Note: The congressman's son began prison sentence immediately after sentencing.]

Rep. Chaka Fattah (D)

Chapter VI

#BlueLivesMatter

"A society that makes war against its police had better learn to make friends with its criminals." – Unknown

Growing up in the inner city, I vividly remember *"Cops and Robbers"* being our favorite pastime. The simplicity of the game — cops represented "good," criminals represented "bad" — reinforced the notion of law and order as a pillar of civilized society. Nowadays, the game of cops and robbers is played differently in the inner city; the robber is the protagonist while the cop is the antagonist. This backward dynamic is a reflection of police being treated as an occupying force while criminals are treated as allies, all because urban America generally views society as a racist quagmire.

For example, in Jackson, MS, which is 74 percent black, Ward 3 councilman Kenneth Stokes proposed a unique crime fighting method for his constituents. He suggested using rocks, bricks, and bottles. However, the recommendation wasn't to use those items against the criminals, but against police from other jurisdictions who chased misdemeanor suspects through Jackson. The councilman claimed that police from surrounding cities put Jackson's children in danger whenever they chase people on neighborhood streets. He also stated:

"What I suggest is we get the black leadership together, and as these jurisdictions come into Jackson we throw rocks and bricks and bottles at them. That will send a message we don't want you in here," he says.

With the potential support of black leadership, this sworn official of Jackson is essentially fighting to give criminals safe passage. This criminal-advocate's rationale unintentionally clarifies why Jackson is number 11 on NeighborhoodScout's lists of *Top 30 Cities with the Highest Murder Rates* and *100 Most Dangerous Cities in the U.S.A.* Despite having a one in 14 chance of victimization by either violent or property crime, and possessing a crime rate that's lower than only two percent of other Mississippi communities, the councilman still feels that having more criminals in Jackson is better than having more police.

Jackson Councilman says 'Let's throw rocks at police'
nbc12.com

In West Memphis (Arkansas), which is ranked number sixteen on NeighborhoodScout's list of *"100 Most Dangerous Cities in the U.S.A,"* and where one's chances of being victimized through violence or property crime are one in 14, the notion of emulating Jackson's usage of *"rocks, bricks, and bottles"* for self-preservation is primitively naive. Instead, the local NAACP wants West Memphis' 63.5 percent black populace to arm themselves. This city, whose crime rate is higher than 97 percent of Arkansas' other cities, is suffocating from urban terrorism. The routine murder of black men didn't sit well with Shabaka Afrika, head of the Crittenden County NAACP, and Hubert Bass, CEO of the Crittenden County Justice Commission. So, they called a news conference. However, this news conference wasn't called to address the urban terrorism in West Memphis; it was called to address the shootings of black men by white officers across the nation.

"We're asking that black people around the country arm themselves and join and establish gun clubs," Bass explained. Afrika expressed, *"Law enforcement has to understand, you cannot do what you please when you see us."*

Reportedly, the motion was centered on self-defense, protecting the black community, and making sure West Memphis does not become another Ferguson. But judging by its crime rate, West Memphis is on its way to becoming another Baltimore or Detroit. Naturally, the RGI doesn't mind that harsh reality — as long as whites can be blamed.

West Memphis NAACP wants black families to arm themselves
wtoc.com

Local leaders want black community to arm themselves
wreg.com

According to the FBI's 2015 Uniform Crime Report, Cincinnati, OH, the "Queen City," had a murder rate of 20.16 per 100,000 residents. Chicago, in comparison, had a murder rate of 15.09 while New York City's murder rate was 3.93 per 100,000. One's chances of becoming a victim of either violent or property crime in

Cincy are one in 15. And within Ohio, more than 98 percent of the communities have a lower crime rate. Consequently, NeighborhoodScout has designated Cincinnati as one of the "*100 Most Dangerous Cities in the U.S.A.*" Obviously, certain residents of the "Queen City" aren't behaving royally these days. This 45 percent black city once had two separate shootings interrupt a peace march. And of course, the collective angst wasn't directed towards Cincy's wrongdoers, it was somehow re-directed towards Cincy's right-doers. *National Review* columnist Heather McDonald captured this urban phenomenon[88]:

"In Cincinnati, a mini-riot broke out when police arrived at the scene of a drive-by shooting on July 30. The drive-by's victims included a four-year-old girl, who was shot in the head. According to an eyewitness, bystanders shouted profanities at the cops, who had started arresting people on outstanding warrants to prevent a retaliatory shooting. The press was assiduously silent about the anti-police chaos. Arrests in other cities, from Baltimore to Los Angeles, can be equally fraught. The four-year-old Cincinnati victim was the second child seriously wounded that month in the city. On July 5, another drive-by left a six-year-old girl paralyzed and partially blind."

I can't think of a place where cops are needed more than in the inner city. Yet, the boys in blue (cops) are treated worse than those other boys in blue (Crips).

Anti-violence march marred by 2 shootings
cincinnati.com

The Anti-Cop Sentiment

Although the RGI is the architect, BLM and its media allies are the driving forces behind today's anti-cop climate; ignoring the normality of black-on-black homicide to chase the anomaly of blue-on-black homicides. This BLM-induced avalanche of destructive propaganda — such as cops are hunting black men — is demonstrably false, but still has effectively appealed to peoples' emotions instead of critical thinking. Even grievance author/journalist Ta-Nehisi Coates, the resurrected James Baldwin to the pro-blacks and current darling of white liberals, revealed his deep-rooted contempt for police in his book, *"Between the World and Me."* He had this to say about the uniformed heroes who died responding to the September 11, terrorist attacks:

"They were not human to me. Black, white, or whatever, they were menaces of nature; they were the fire, the comet, the storm, which could — with no justification — shatter my body."

A Kentucky student created this painting for a high school project and according to a teacher, was a good example how *"racial violence has evolved."*

Patrisse Cullors, a co-founder of Black Lives Matter, wants to further capitalize on this deception by building a national network of communities to respond to law enforcement violence. She has already received a $500,000 "racial justice grant" from Google to help make her scheme a reality. *KQED* news highlighted Cullors' initiative:

"We know what to do if an earthquake happens in California. People know what to do if a tornado happens. But what happens when your loved one is killed by the police? When your loved one is killed in a jail cell?" Cullors says.

"We don't know what to do. We've seen it time and time again. Families are at a loss. They don't know who to talk to, they don't know who to go to because, you don't go to your murderer to have them give you justice."

Black and brown communities can't rely on law enforcement to protect black and brown bodies, says Cullors.

"If your loved one is harmed or killed by law enforcement, if they're illegally arrested, if there's a raid on your home, you will be able to call a hotline number that will be staffed 24/7 that can help you navigate the system."

What makes her idea different is that the rapid responders will be people who live in the community and understand what it's like to face law enforcement violence firsthand.

"It will be a multiracial justice team. Allies can definitely play a role. But really the point is people who are directly impacted, and that often looks like black and brown people, and poor people."

She imagines the first responders could help victims file a complaint against the police. And if the complaint isn't getting attention, they could help stage a protest in the neighborhood or organize to demand that the officer is fired.

The article neglected to mention that BLM doesn't have an established hotline number for urban residents who've been victimized by black thugs — which is far more probable. Oh, I guess those residents will have to continue to use the number that already exists... 911. Certainly, BLM uses it.

Black Lives Matter Co-Founder's Plan to Reduce Law Enforcement Violence
ww2.kqed.org

The seemingly ubiquitous axiom that cops are racists has led to this age where non-compliance during police engagement is an encouraged strategy; e.g., Eric Garner and Freddie Gray. Undoubtedly, the motive is financial since filing frivolous civil suits against cops for a financial settlement has become a new lottery system. However, confrontation instead of compliance will continue to lead to fatal consequences, and that's what BLM gleefully envisions.

The Other White Meat

Historically, pork has been the other white meat, but in this anti-cop atmosphere, white officers have become the other white meat — and they're always ripe for consumption. BLM's anti-cop chants have evolved from — *"What do we want? Dead cops. When do we want it? Now!"* and *"Pigs in a blanket, fry 'em like bacon"* — to actual black-on-blue violence. A "kill them before they kill us" mentality is in effect. And like black-on-black crime, black-on-blue crime is ignored and even excused.

Video Shows NYC Protesters Chanting for "Dead Cops"
nbcnewyork.com

Black Lives Matter organizer stands by group's chant to cook police officers like 'pigs in a blanket' and 'fry 'em like bacon'
dailymail.co.uk

"Putting Wings on Pigs"

In December 2014, Ismaaiyl Brinsley, a 28-year-old BLM supporter, and proud thug, had an insatiable appetite for the other white meat. So, he went hunting. Before leaving the house, he posted his intentions on Instagram — a social network. This hunting trip would be in retaliation for the deaths of Eric Garner and Michael Brown. The menace to society, whose nineteen arrests spanned multiple states, wrote:

"I'm Putting Wings On Pigs Today. They Take 1 Of Ours...... Let's Take 2 of Theirs #ShootThePolice #RIPErivGardner #RipMikeBown This May Be My Final Post ********** I'm Putting Pigs In A Blanket"

Two witnesses told police that Brinsley approached them on the street in Brooklyn, asked if they had gang affiliations, told them to follow him on Instagram, and then said, *"Watch what I'm going to do."* Shortly thereafter, Brinsley ambushed New York Police Department officers Rafael Ramos and Wenjian Liu while they were eating lunch inside their patrol car outside a Brooklyn housing project. He fired four shots through the passenger side window killing them both then fled to a nearby subway station, where he cowardly shot and killed himself.

The urban terrorist followed through on his threat to put *"wings on pigs."*

Post #1 is from Ismaaiyl Brinsley: *"We Don't Respect The Pigs, That's Why The Camera Is His (Sic) In His Face. And Turn The Music Up When He's Talking"*

Post #2 is from a sicko supporter: *"Ismaaiyl Brinsley is forever a hood hero ...this nigga will never be forgotten...RIP homie"*

Should've Killed More Cops?

The family of 23-year-old Melvin Santiago remembers his dream of becoming a cop. Through hard work, focus, and commitment, his dream materialized. Knowing the associated risks, he wanted to work the West District of Jersey City, also known as the *"Wild, Wild West."* Santiago's stepdad, who raised him from age nine, asked the young cop if he feared dying on the street. *"Well,"* the officer replied, *"at least if something happened to me, being a cop, at least I go for a good cause."* Unfortunately, something did happen to him; something tragic that prevented him from reaching his one year anniversary. The rookie officer was ambushed and executed by Lawrence Campbell, an urban terrorist who also had a dream — a dream to become famous by killing cops.

Shortly after 4 a.m., Officer Melvin Santiago and other patrol units responded to a report of an armed robbery at a 24-hour Walgreens drugstore. The store, which has a security guard because of the area's high rate of crime, is only blocks from a notoriously crime-ridden, gang-infested neighborhood. Unbeknownst to the officers, Campbell had beaten and stabbed the store's security guard, before stealing his gun during the assault. The urban terrorist then waited outside for police to arrive. While waiting, he inexplicably apologized to a customer for his criminality in the store, and then announced, *"Watch the news later, I'm going to be famous!"*

When the cops arrived a few minutes later, Campbell quickly unleashed a barrage of bullets, leaving a string of thirteen holes across the windshield of officer Santiago's patrol car. Santiago, who was wearing a bulletproof vest, was killed before he could even exit the vehicle. He was shot in the head with what turned out to be the security guard's 9mm semi-automatic weapon. Officers returned fired hitting Campbell multiple times. He was pronounced dead at the scene. A witness said that Campbell had no plans to rob the store; he wanted to kill police so that he could become famous.

Officer Santiago's cruiser

Admittedly, part one of Campbell's kamikaze mission was successful, but would his final despicable act make this career felon — who was also wanted for questioning regarding a recent Jersey City homicide — famous as he envisioned, or infamous?

Only in the "hood" would a certified savage like Campbell be glorified, which is why a sidewalk shrine featuring an assortment of lit candles, balloons, and empty liquor bottles was created in his honor. The memorial's main attraction was duct taped to a wall above the candles and liquor bottles — two white tee shirts bearing handwritten messages from supporters. Some of the words of encouragement were, *"REAL NIGGAZ DONT DIE,"* *"FOREVER A 'G,' "SEE U ON THE OTHER SIDE," "GONE BUT NOT FORGOTTEN," "REST EASY,"* and *"THUG IN PEACE."* Ironically, the shrine was illegally erected under a conspicuous sign that implicitly stated in capital letters, *"PRIVATE PROPERTY, NO TRESPASSING, NO GATHERING, JCPD"* Just as Campbell ignored laws while living, the mourners fittingly ignored the *"PRIVATE PROPERTY, NO TRESPASSING, NO GATHERING,* law to honor his death.

The urban terrorist was correct... he became famous

At the impromptu memorial, the dead thug's wife told local reporters that she only wished her husband had killed more officers before they gunned him down.

"If that's the case, he should've took more with him. If they was going to stand over my husband and shoot him like a f---ing dog, he should've took all of them the f--- out. Sorry for the officer's family. That's, you know, whatever. But, at the end of the day, [Lawrence] got a family, too. All they care about is the officer. That's how I feel. God forgive me, but that's how I feel."

She later tried to retract some of her words, saying, "I do apologize. I was very angry." But she still maintained her criticism of the cops, complaining, *"They called an ambulance for the officer — why didn't they call an ambulance for Lawrence?"*

Man who executed rookie cop: 'I'm going to be famous'
nypost.com

Disgust at cop-killer's memorial BIGGER than shrine to officer he shot - as his widow says she wishes he'd killed MORE police
dailymail.co.uk

Cop killer's widow rages: He should've killed more cops
nypost.com

It's the Cop's Fault?

Call me old-fashioned, but I'm a staunch believer that family cookouts shouldn't end with shootouts against cops. Evidently, 25-year-old, career-criminal Major Davis Jr. thought differently — which best explains his decision for bringing an AK-47 type rifle to the post-Fourth of July gathering.

When Indianapolis police responded to a call about a man with a gun, and shots being fired in the vicinity, they arrived to find Davis wielding a rifle. Officials said Davis Jr. was *"obviously upset."* After refusing orders to put down the gun — that was pointed at Officer Perry Renn — a three to five-minute gun battle ensued, leaving Davis Jr. critically wounded, and Officer Renn dead. Indianapolis Metropolitan Police Department Chief Rick Hite wondered how a family cookout could turn so deadly. Chief Hite pondered:

"Why would he be in that area, at that time, at that cookout with that weapon?" Why wasn't he joining the rest of his family and the rest of the community in the spirit of peace?"

The family neglected to answer that valid question during a *WISH-TV News 8* interview; instead, they made excuses for the thug's actions and even blamed the police.

The family of Major Davis Jr., the man accused of killing Officer Perry Renn, is speaking out about the shooting. His aunt, cousins and his children's grandmother all talked to 24-Hour News 8 on Sunday afternoon.

The family is still struggling to accept that Davis Jr. could be a part of something like this. He is a father with four children, ages 10 and under. His family has had a long, tense history with Indianapolis police officers.

"You don't know what he been through with IMPD. We do. He's scarred for life," said his children's grandmother, Pam Moornan.

The Davis family's history with police began with Major Davis Sr. He served at least three years on a drug conviction and was arrested again in 2003 for public intoxication.

He died of a heart attack in police custody when Davis Jr. was a young teen. Though the coroner's report said the officers weren't at fault for any fatal injuries, the family still holds officers responsible.

"He wasn't a bad person. His father was killed by IMPD. That is enough to hurt a person and scar him for life," said Moornan.

One of the officers listed in that 2003 police report is Officer Perry Renn.

"I imagine he figured they were going to try and kill him. I mean cause look what they did to his father," said Moornan.

On Saturday night, the family says they were having a cookout.

"Next thing, I just heard shots and everybody running in the house and everybody hit the floor," said Yvonne Moornan, Davis Jr.'s aunt.

By the time they got outside, they realized those shots were Davis Jr. and Officer Renn shooting at each other. Davis had an assault rifle.

"Major is not a bad person in spite of what happened. Things happen," said Pam Moornan.

Now, the Davis family is worried about their son's reputation and again, questioning police tactics.

TALEEB STARKES   **129**

"It's horrible about what took place, but, I mean, I don't think it's fair though for them to keep dragging him through the mud," said Moornan.

And again, questioning police tactics.

"I don't know how the police was shooting. I don't know if they took concern of any kids running around," said Yvonne Moornan.

The family did say it is sorry for Officer Renn's family, but they said the tragedy may have been avoided if Officer Renn would've stayed at his car since he could see Davis had a gun.

Blaming officers despite the facts is a BLM-inspired attribute. It's asinine. Obviously, the concept of accountability is lost upon the family. Some say it's victim-blaming. No, it's not victim-blaming! Davis Jr. isn't the victim; Officer Perry Renn is the victim.

Murder suspect's family speaks out about shooting

wishtv.com

Officer Perry Renn

As previously mentioned, BLM has also inspired a new wave of litigiousness. While waiting for trial for Officer Renn's murder — in which prosecutors want the death penalty — Davis Jr. filed a federal lawsuit against the late officer and others for $2.3 million dollars, claiming *"excessive deadly force"* was used against him. Additionally, he, according to the claim *"has been and will continue to be irreparably injured by the misconduct of the defendants,"* and alleges that the injuries resulted in neurological and digestive problems that caused him to be confined to a wheelchair. Davis Jr., who is representing himself, claims Officer Renn shot him eleven times at close range as he walked unarmed in an alley to his van. He alleges that there's no evidence he was armed during the encounter. In the complaint, he also stated that fireworks were going off at the time, and they *"added to the confusion."*

There's a reason why the old adage, *"He who represents himself has a fool for a client"* maintains validity. This fool actually claimed that he wasn't armed! In spite of the ballistics, his girlfriend's frantic 911 call saying, *"The police just shot my (expletive) boyfriend" and "They shot each other,"* and the most damning piece of evidence of all; Officer Renn is dead! Major Davis Jr. is a major idiot, but rational according to BLM standards.

Accused killer of IMPD officer Perry Renn sues cop for $2.3 million
indystar.com

Shooting Police is OK?

In Milwaukee, a woman was sitting in a car waiting for her brother when a thug jumped inside the vehicle, put a gun to her neck, and then demanded the car keys. She told the gunman that she didn't have the keys (she was sitting in the passenger's seat). He responded, *"I want all the money or I'm going to shoot you."* She immediately surrendered her wallet and he exited the vehicle. Less than a week later, officers were investigating a burglary when this same urban terrorist jumped into a stolen vehicle that was under surveillance. As he commenced to drive, officers approached the vehicle *"effectively blocking it from moving — drew their weapons — and ordered the defendant to stop and surrender,"* according to the police report. The thug refused to comply and ran from the scene. While being chased, he pulled out a handgun and fired several shots at the officers in pursuit. Detective Jeffrey Griffin was wounded and hospitalized with *"significant internal injuries."* A massive, all-night manhunt ensued — with the cop shooter's name and face prominently highlighted by the local media. The Milwaukee K-9 unit found him hiding in a friend's basement closet, under a pile of debris. It's appropriate that trash would hide amongst the trash. He was taken into custody without incident.

Det. Griffin was also shot in 1999 as a Milwaukee patrolman

Colleen Henry, a *WISN 12 News* reporter, interviewed the head of the home to find out why the fugitive was allowed to stay there. *"He's a good friend of ours. I'm not going to throw him down. I'm not going to throw him to the wolves,"* said Stephanie King, who added that she's known the cop shooter since he was little; he's friends with her kids. She also confirmed that she saw his picture on television that morning. *"And did you say you better get out of here?"* the reporter asked. *"No, I did not,"* King responded. *"And they didn't arrest you or anything for harboring a fugitive?"* asked the reporter. *"No, cause I ain't harboring no fugitive,"* King replied. *"Cause to me, he didn't do no wrong. He just shot a cop and then everybody come around when they shoot the cop, but when the cops shoot people do they come around?"* King said.

There will always be friction between those who enforce the law and those who break the law. But when members of the community steadfastly fight for criminals, the criminal element wins while the community loses.

Man accused of shooting Wauwatosa detective charged with armed robbery
wisn.com

Deal reached: Najee Harmon pleads guilty in shooting of Wauwatosa detective
fox6now.com

PC Politics > Police

Many police departments and politicians have decided to pacify the RGI at the expense of public safety. For example, after the Michael Brown and Eric Garner grand jury decisions, Philadelphia's mayor at the time, Michael Nutter, created an eight-minute video lecture[89] for police officers. During the video, Mayor Nutter urged officers to build trust with community members, and use force only when "absolutely necessary." For three consecutive days, Philly's finest were mandated to watch his condescending video before hitting the urban streets of "Killadelphia," where no-snitching is gospel, and cops are typically viewed as a nemesis.

During a week's span in 2013, the Philadelphia Police Department experienced seven police-involved shootings[90] that resulted in the deaths of four culprits. Despite the fact that six of those shootings involved gun-toting suspects and the seventh involved a knife-wielding man who charged at officers, Philadelphia's mayor had no desire to make a video urging citizens to comply with police commands. As an alternative, the police brass humiliated its frontline cops by publically apologizing for the deadly outcomes. Such political correctness and appeasement exhibited by the police brass only empower felons like Isaac Carmichael[91], whose encounter with the Philadelphia Police occurred a week after the department expressed remorse for the previous seven shootings.

Carmichael, who had three previous convictions, including two for firearms violations, and who fits the description of an urban terrorist as defined in my book *The Un-Civil War,* fired at a woman and her companions on a busy street for rejecting his advances. Officers in the vicinity chased Carmichael, who then fired shots at them during the pursuit. Amazingly, he was apprehended without police returning fire, and no officers or civilians were injured. The police brass was quick to tout this encounter as an example of police restraint. Cops are now expected to blow kisses at armed threats instead of blowing them away.

More PC Madness

Blacks and Muslims are amongst groups treated as a protected class. Any negative comment about them in any capacity is political suicide for public officials in liberal-controlled cities. So, imagine the quandary faced by Philadelphia's newly elected Mayor Jim Kenney — who was barely a week into his first term — when a black Muslim shot an unsuspecting cop on patrol.

On January 7, 2016, Officer Jesse Hartnett was on routine patrol when a black man dressed in a white, long-sleeved tunic — traditional Muslim garb — walked towards the marked cruiser at the crosswalk appearing to ask for directions. It was a ploy. The perp pulled out a 9mm gun and unleashed 13 shots at the sitting duck officer. Surveillance camera footage showed him continuing to fire as he reached inside the lowered driver's side window. Officer Hartnett was hit three times but managed to exit his patrol car and return fire at the suspect — hitting him three times. *"Shots fired!... I'm bleeding heavily!"* the injured officer shouted over the radio. *"I'm bleeding. Get us another unit out here!"* Officers quickly swarmed to his location and apprehended the shooter a block away; the smoking 9mm Glock 17 that can hold 17 rounds in a standard magazine was still in his possession. Turns out, it was a stolen police firearm.

4-year veteran Officer Jesse Hartnett

The black Muslim confessed to the crime and declared, *"I follow Allah. I pledge my allegiance to the Islamic state, and that's why I did what I did."* Police Commissioner Richard Ross said the perp believes that the police defend laws that are contrary to the teachings of the Quran. When asked about the shooting at a news conference, Mayor Kenney responded:

"In no way shape or form does anyone in this room believe that Islam or the teaching of Islam has anything to do with what you've seen on the screen. It is abhorrent. It is terrible and it does not represent the religion in any way, shape or form or any of its teachings. This is a criminal with a stolen gun who tried to kill one of our officers. It has nothing to do with being a Muslim or following the Islamic faith."

The short version of this story: Muslim shooter says, *"I'm a terrorist for ISIS."* Mayor forcefully responds, *"No you're not!*

You're a disenfranchised minority suffering from post-traumatic slavery disorder! This incident is not your fault... It's society's fault!" #BlackMuslimVotesMatter

Cops: Suspect Says He Shot Officer In Name Of Islam
philadelphia.cbslocal.com

Mayor Kenney On Officer Shooting: 'It Has Nothing To Do With Being Muslim'
philadelphia.cbslocal.com

The Black Muslim approached the cruiser and fired 12 shots

In 2012, the city of Omaha unfathomably accounted for nearly 80 percent of Nebraska's homicides, and that harrowing statistic has remained steady in subsequent years. Most of the homicides disproportionately occurred in northeast Omaha (which is predominantly black), including the drive-by murder of five-year-old Payton Benson[92] shot while eating breakfast on a living room couch. Overall, blacks are only 13.7 percent of Omaha's population.

5-year-old Payton Benson

Omaha.com reported:

"[O]maha's streets in recent years have become among the deadliest places in America for blacks. Fueled by gun violence in northeast Omaha, Nebraska has the third-highest black homicide rate in the nation, according to the latest compilation of detailed national homicide statistics."

When Omaha's white police chief, was asked to speculate on why an overwhelming majority of Nebraska's homicides were clustered in northeast Omaha, he responded, *"I don't see what purpose that serves."* In other words, political correctness trumps public safety. His protectionism of black thug culture run amok wasn't reciprocated by Ernie Chambers, Nebraska's longest serving state senator (also black) who represents high-crime north Omaha. The senator compared American police to Islamic terrorists and submitted he'd shoot a cop if he had a weapon. State Sen. Ernie Chambers said during a legislative hearing on gun bills that you don't have to go halfway around the world to find an ISIS mentality. It can be found in America because police terrorize blacks every day — as reported by NebraskaWatchdog.org. *"My ISIS is the police,"* Chambers said, adding police can get away with shooting people if they "think" they're going to do something — like pull a weapon. *"The police are licensed to kill us — children, old people,"* he alleged. Then, Chambers' rhetoric escalated, saying if he had a gun, he would use it on police, not his political opponents.

"If I was going to carry a weapon, it wouldn't be against you, it wouldn't be against these people who come here that I might have a dispute with. Mine would be for the police. And if I carried a gun I'd want to shoot him first and then ask questions later, like they say the cop ought to do."

Unlike Omaha's police chief, I'll say why the city's violence is concentrated in certain areas. Quite simply, the violence is undeniably linked to a sociopathic subculture that infests urban areas. There's an unholy matrimony between thugs and thug enablers. However, Omaha's inner-city quandary isn't unique; this trend dominates America's urban landscapes.

Officers' Morale

Police officer Arik Matson once opined, *"Police officers may drive black and white cars, however, what goes on in their job is a lot of gray."* This truism is expected to be lost upon civilians, but when politicians and police brass themselves lose sight of this fact, officer morale plummets. With the anti-police sentiment and

---

the political pandering of police brass, officers' lack of morale and enthusiasm is being felt nationwide. Police simply do not want to become the next headline, thrown under the bus, or scapegoated for simply doing their job. The thin blue line has become a tightrope that all officers are walking. Thus, arrests are trending downward. In the first three months of 2015, Chicago police stopped and searched 157,346 people for suspicious behavior. This year, that number dropped to 20,908 — down 86 percent[93]. Also, the passing of an American Civil Liberties Union-influenced law to combat racial profiling now requires the police to fill out up to 60 pages of forms for each stop. Chicago's Mayor Rahm Emanuel noticed the trend and stated that the CPD had gone "fetal." In a city that typically has more homicides than days in a calendar year, the Chicago Tribune[94] captured the CPD's dispirited attitude:

"Some fear being put under a microscope more than ever for actions they take on the street. They worry about getting into trouble even for treating people appropriately. As a result, unless they're responding to 911 calls, they're less likely to make street stops on their own, even if their gut tells them someone is up to no good, they said. "The days of the hunch are over," said a sergeant with 20 years' experience who works on the South Side. "You have to have something more than intuition."

Arrests in Chicago

January 2011	11,962
January 2012	11,657
January 2013	11,613
January 2014	9,489
January 2015	9,969
January 2016	6,818

Source: Chicago Police Department   @ChiTribGraphics

The results of Chicago's public servants being forced to serve their own interests

After the Baltimore tsunami erupted in April 2015, Baltimore's arrests dropped 60 percent the following month, compared with arrests the previous year. In New York City, arrests plummeted 66 percent as the nation's largest police force turned a blind eye to some minor crimes, and made arrests only *"when they have to"* — according to the New York Post. This pattern of police disengagement exposed the damaged relationship between the

NYPD and Mayor Bill de Blasio's administration; officers felt betrayed by the mayor's political correctness.

Arrests plummet 66% with NYPD in virtual work stoppage

nypost.com

POLICE ACTION	2013	2014	CHANGE
Criminal Court summonses	4,831	300	Down 94%
Traffic violations	10,069	587	Down 94%
Parking violations	14,699	1,241	Down 92%
Overall arrests	5,370	1,820	Down 66%

A result of the NYPD blues

The Ferguson Effect

The lack of morale has resulted in a condition of stagnation commonly referred to as the "Ferguson effect" — cops intentionally standing down on the job to avoid potential encounters out of fear of demonization. The Ferguson effect has been cited as the reason for violent spikes in cities nationwide. Even in racially diverse places such as Providence, Rhode Island, a conspicuous change is surfacing between cops and the communities they serve.

"On the streets, where Maj. Tom Verdi spent the early days of his nearly three decades on the force, the respectful nods of acknowledgement have been replaced with some "hostile" stares. And within the ethnically mixed South Side, Lt. Henry Remolina said the black and white uniform often renders him a stranger in the very neighborhood where he grew up.

There is no tying the tension here to any specific confrontation gone bad. No shooting, no beating captured on video. Rather, it is akin, law enforcement officials and community leaders said, to a powerful aftershock that has reignited long-unresolved social grievances in Providence and in many other cities across the country following the wave of civil unrest that swept through Ferguson, Albuquerque, Baltimore, Chicago, Cleveland, North Charleston, S.C., and Staten Island."

This strategy of policing by non-policing, which leads to a police force that's reactive instead of proactive, is exactly what the RGI wants.

Self-Defense is Racist?

This Ferguson-effect nearly cost an Alabama detective his life. The plainclothes detective was en route to investigate a string of burglaries when he saw a GMC Yukon erratically driving on the interstate. After pulling over the SUV, he called for backup and commanded the man to stay inside the vehicle. Backup was called so that the detective could continue his burglary investigation while another officer handled the traffic stop. While waiting for backup, the man exited the car, aggressively approached the detective, and repeatedly questioned why he'd been pulled over. The detective considered using force but considered the potential backlash. *"A lot of officers are being too cautious because of what's going on in the media,"* he told CNN. *"I hesitated because I didn't want to be in the media like I am right now."* The man, a 34-year-old convicted felon, grabbed the detective's gun and pistol-whipped him until the detective lost consciousness. The last thing the officer remembered was getting sucker-punched in a parking lot then waking up in a hospital bed with staples in his head. He suffered multiple lacerations to his head and face. He didn't shoot the man because of the outcry surrounding a spate of police shootings nationally. *"We don't want to be in the media,"* the detective said. *"It's hard times right now for us."* The thug was captured and charged with attempted murder.

Shortly after the brutal confrontation, pictures of the bloodied officer lying unconscious on a sidewalk in a parking lot surfaced on social media. And he was taunted and mocked by the anti-cop mob online while the perp was celebrated. Birmingham police Sgt. Heath Boackle, president of the Fraternal Order of Police, told AI.com:

"He was laying there lifeless and people were standing around taking pictures. If the tables were turned, and that was a suspect lying there, they would be rioting. If the officer would have shot him, then he would have shot an 'unarmed man.' Instead, he took the gun from the officer. The officer had every right to shoot him. We're lucky we're not talking about him killing the officer."

This black-on-blue crime left the officer beaten until he was black and blue. Had this detective defended himself, he would've most certainly have become the next Darren Wilson and Birmingham the next Ferguson. Ever notice how citizens make it their business to videotape cops but never do the same to the thugs terrorizing their communities?

Man charged in Birmingham detective's beating; outrage follows support of attack on social media
al.com

Pistol-whipped detective says he didn't shoot attacker because of headlines
cnn.com

Post #1: *"Pistol whipped his ass to sleep"* hashtag *"#FckDaPolice"*
Post #2: *"Pistol pimped his faced n um chillen now"*

According to the FBI, 48,315 officers were assaulted while performing their duties in 2014[95]; the largest percentage of victim officers (30.8 percent) were assaulted while responding to disturbance calls. In urban America, disturbance calls along with traffic pursuits/stops, are typically the most dangerous situations for police. And with relations presently strained between cops and inner-city residents, I'm surprised that the police even respond to calls in neighborhoods where the maelstrom of criticism is never lodged against the menacing malefactors but cops. Without a doubt, this reality eventually affects the cops' psyche, and may ultimately create cynicism or a hardened heart. After all, officers aren't machines but unfairly expected to operate emotionlessly like machines.

Blue-On-Black Deaths

Whenever a blue-on-black death occurs, no context or fact-finding mission is necessary — a black person being shot by a cop is the only context and fact needed. But, are black deaths encountered during police encounters a manifestation of police prejudice, or disproportionate black criminality? According to a Rasmussen poll conducted in March 2015, 56 percent of black voters believe that discrimination against minorities is a bigger problem than the crime levels in low-income inner-city communities. Undeniably, the consistently high crime rate in black communities results in frequent blue-on-black encounters; specifically, blue encounters with black criminals. However, this unavoidable reality doesn't eclipse the vast amount of criminality that's suffocating urban areas. Those 56 percent black poll voters must have been black criminals themselves or apologists for the criminals. Apologists disingenuously stress the lie that blue-on-black victimization is sanctioned by the state; when, in actuality, black-on-black victimization is sanctioned by the state... the *state of denial* within the black community.

Bigger Problem - Racist Cops or Inner City Crime?
rasmussenreports.com

The following chart documents the FBI's 2014 arrest rate for Blacks, Asians, and Whites — Hispanics are lumped into the White category by the Feds, thus inflating the numbers.

Arrest Percentages - 2014

Offense	Whites	Blacks	Asians
Murder & Non-Negligent Manslaughter	46.3	51.3	1.3
Rape	67.2	29.9	1.4
Robbery	42.3	55.9	0.8
Aggravated Assault	63.7	33.1	1.5
Burglary	67.6	30.2	1.1
Larceny-theft	69.1	28.0	1.2
Motor Vehicle theft	66.5	30.7	1.3
Arson	73.1	23.4	1.3
Violent Crime*	59.4	37.7	1.4
Property Crime**	68.8	28.4	1.2
Other Assaults	65.4	31.9	1.1
Forgery & Counterfeiting	63.8	34.0	1.5
Fraud	66.1	31.8	1.0
Embezzlement	61.9	35.6	1.7
Stolen Property; Buying, Receiving, Possessing	65.5	32.2	1.2

Vandalism	70.1	27.0	1.0
Weapons; carrying, possessing, etc.	57.3	40.7	1.2
Prostitution & Commercialized Vice	53.7	41.8	3.9
Sex Offenses (except Rape & Prostitution)	72.5	24.3	1.6
Drug Abuse Violations	68.9	29.1	1.1
Gambling	35.8	58.9	4.4
Offenses Against Family & Children	64.4	32.9	0.7
Driving Under the Influence	83.7	13.0	1.8
Liquor Laws	80.2	14.5	1.3
Drunkedness	80.9	15.7	1.1
Disorderly Conduct	63.0	33.9	0.7
Vagrancy	68.7	28.3	0.8
All other Offenses (Except Traffic)	67.8	29.5	0.9
Suspicions	52.7	44.7	1.2
Curfew & Loitering Law Violations	51.4	46.2	1.1
Total Percent	69.4	27.8	1.1

*Violent crimes are offenses of murder, non-negligent manslaughter, rape, robbery, & aggravated assault.
**Property crimes are offenses of burglary, larceny,-theft, motor vehicle theft, and arson.

The *"Driving Under the Influence"* (DUI) rate of 13 percent, is the only category where crime is proportional to black's national population percent. The arrest rates for the other crimes — major and minor — are disproportionally high. And as long as black crime rates remain disproportionate, cops will be disproportionately deployed in black communities. Since the feds lumped Hispanics in with whites, the breakdown of proportional crimes is complicated. Census.gov states that whites (alone, not Hispanic or Latino) are 62 percent, Hispanics/Latinos (alone) are 17 percent of the national populace — whites and Hispanics (who identify as white) are 77 percent. Even if I use 77 percent as the benchmark, whites are still underrepresented in most categories, especially the major violent categories. Asians, 5.4 percent of the national population, are also underrepresented in all categories. It's evident that different races commit crimes at different rates, — in other words, *"Other races do it too"* — but only blacks are determined to contribute more than their 13 percent share. Furthermore, cops — of all races — are also disproportionately endangered by black assailants. Over the past decade, forty-percent of cop killers have been black, and officers are killed by blacks at a rate 2.5 times higher than the rate at which blacks are killed by police —according to Wall Street Journal.[96]

Sure, it's trendy to assume that every black person shot by police is the true victim, but even when shootings are justified, BLM insists that police are assassinating blacks who were simply planting daisies in the community's garden.

For example, in Raleigh, NC, 24-year-old Akiel Denkins was shot in the back seven times — by a white cop — while climbing a fence to evade capture. The head of the North Carolina NAACP implored the authorities to conduct a fair and transparent investigation into the fatal police shooting, and during a news conference stated that someone running away is not a *"license to kill."* A woman who asked not to be identified told the local news that the foot chase started when a man (Denkins) took off as he was approached by a police officer. The man (Denkins) ignored the officer's demands to stop, the woman said, and the chase went over one fence and turned deadly after a second fence. *"When they got to the tall fence, the boy (Denkins) jumped the tall fence, but the police couldn't,"* the woman said. *"When the police went to jump over the tall fence, he fell. When he fell, he just started shooting his gun."* Local television coverage showed police forming a line in the street as a crowd of approximately one hundred people gathered at the scene of the shooting behind yellow crime tape and began chanting, *"Black lives matter,"* and *"No justice, no peace!"* Some people shouted obscenities at the officers. *"They killed my son for no reason,"* said the victim's grieving mother. *"Everybody out here said he was running, didn't have a gun, (was) trying to jump a fence, and that officer shot my son seven times. For what? For nothing."* Local media outlet WRAL captured more community reactions:

Denkins was well-known in the community. He had two sons, ages 3 and 2, was working on his GED through the Neighbor to Neighbor program and hoped to become a carpenter.

"He could have been my son. I treated him like my son. I've fed him at my church before. Now, he's lying back there dead," said Rev. Chris Jones, pastor of Ship of Zion Church, which is about four blocks from the shooting scene.

Crowds of people milled about amid the dozen or so police cruisers that blocked off the neighborhood as investigators spent much of the afternoon collecting evidence and witness statements from the shooting scene.

"The mood around here is more along the lines of people are just frustrated, angry, upset and disappointed," said Casanova Womack, who lives in the neighborhood. "A lot of guys around here are saying what you've probably heard before – 'Why call the cops if the cops won't even come down?' and 'Instead of protect and serve, kill.'"

Jones was among several clergy members who tried to quell anger in the crowd, but he said he is disheartened by the shooting.

"It's going to damage the relationship with police," Jones said. "Even I have to fear. Even me, because of my color, now I've got to fear, when before I had a great relationship with officers."

Jones said that Denkins did not have to die.

"If he ran from you today, you could have arrested him tomorrow. Why did you have to kill him today," he said.

Monday night, hundreds gathered in the streets not far from where Denkins was killed.

"He's gone. Why? Because of the color of his skin," said Minister Brenda Ginger.

There were tears, signs, and candles as people held a vigil before marching through the streets, but there was also growing outrage in the crowd.

"We are sick and tired of being sick and tired," said Ginger. "It is time for change. It is time for all of us to get together and say no to the injustice."

While the shooting brought the crowd together, some of the emotion felt Monday night came from a deeper place and had been building for some time.

"They want to lock you up as a modern-day slave," said community leader Diana Powell. "This is a very defining moment."

Police: Officer who shot, killed drug suspect is 29-year-old senior officer
wral.com

Indeed, this is a tragic story — especially if you're a fan of race-based fiction. Personally, I prefer science fiction, not race-based fiction, but hey, to each his own. The true sequence of events was revealed in the official police report[97], which Raleigh's black police chief submitted to the mayor and city council. It read, in part:

Shortly before noon on February 29, 2016, Senior Officer D.C. Twiddy was on Bragg Street near Mangum Street when he observed an individual he recognized as Mr. Akiel Rakim Lakeith Denkins. Officer Twiddy was aware that Mr. Denkins had an outstanding warrant for his arrest relating to felony drug charges. Officer Twiddy, who was in uniform, parked his marked patrol vehicle facing south on Mangum Street, got out and began to approach Mr. Denkins who had turned and already begun to walk away. When Officer Twiddy told Mr. Denkins to stop, he began to run west on Bragg Street before turning North on South East Street, with Officer

Twiddy chasing him on foot. Mr. Denkins made a sharp right and ran between two houses on South East Street. Officer Twiddy slipped and fell on loose gravel as he attempted to follow. As Officer Twiddy was getting up to continue the pursuit, he observed Mr. Denkins jump a fence and continue toward the back of the house located at 1117 South East Street. Officer Twiddy jumped the fence and continued the chase. As he came around a north-east corner of the house, he saw Mr. Denkins who was attempting to climb over a second fence. Mr. Denkins stopped and turned toward Officer Twiddy.

Officer Twiddy ran to and grabbed Mr. Denkins, in an effort to take him into custody. While the two struggled, Officer Twiddy felt Mr. Denkins reaching for an object in the front of his waistband. As the struggle continued, Officer Twiddy observed Mr. Denkins start to pull a handgun from the front of his waistband and begin to move it toward Officer Twiddy.

While still struggling with Mr. Denkins, Officer Twiddy drew his duty weapon and fired multiple shots as Mr. Denkins continued to move the firearm in his direction. After the first shots were fired, Officer Twiddy felt Mr. Denkins' hand or arm make contact with his duty weapon. Officer Twiddy, fearing that Mr. Denkins was either going to shoot him or attempt to take his duty weapon, stepped back and fired additional shots at Mr. Denkins, who still had the firearm in his hand. Mr. Denkins collapsed to the ground, dropping the firearm in the process. Officer Twiddy then used his police radio to call for assistance. Additional police units arrived on the scene as well as Emergency Medical Services personnel, who pronounced Mr. Denkins deceased.

The report also noted that *"The handgun located at the scene, which had been in Mr. Denkins' possession during the encounter, had been reported stolen on January 31, 2016."* The preliminary autopsy not only showed that he was shot four times — not seven as claimed — but the shots hit his right chest, left forearm, right upper arm, and right shoulder — not in his back, as claimed. Despite the fact that Denkins had been arrested sixteen times on twenty-six charges since 2011, with charges including assault, resisting officers, carrying a concealed gun and possession with intent to sell and distribute cocaine, his death by white cop still qualified him for martyrdom. Unfortunately for BLM, the non-fiction version didn't fit their *"killed because of skin color,"* narrative, but facts rarely do. Yet again, the wise and timeless sentiment expressed by President Calvin Coolidge comes to mind: *"I sometimes wish that people would put a little more emphasis upon the observance of the law than they do upon its enforcement."*

POLICE: Man pulled gun before being shot by Raleigh officer
witn.com

Are there rogue cops who dishonor the badge and betray the public's trust? Absolutely, and most cops would agree. The cops who don't agree are probably the problem. However, judge any alleged criminality or ethics violations on a case by case basis, and if the claims of criminality are confirmed, make the disgraced cop walk the plank. It's outright wrong and completely idiotic to throw the entire force overboard for an individual officer's offenses. One bad apple doesn't spoil the batch, and black people — of all people — routinely apply this same logic when conversations of disproportionate black criminality occur. Society is fully capable of holding cops responsible for their wrongdoings, but BLM doesn't really want to use that approach. Its relevancy depends on being the judge and jury.

Blue-on-White Deaths

Contradictory to popular opinion, more whites are killed during police encounters than blacks — even though blacks maintain disproportionately high arrest rates. According to an op-ed from Manhattan Institute Fellow Heather Mac Donald:

"The Washington Post has been gathering data on fatal police shootings over the past year and a half to correct acknowledged deficiencies in federal tallies. The emerging data should open many eyes.

For starters, fatal police shootings make up a much larger proportion of white and Hispanic homicide deaths than black homicide deaths. According to the Post database, in 2015 officers killed 662 whites and Hispanics, and 258 blacks. (The overwhelming majority of all those police-shooting victims were attacking the officer, often with a gun.) Using the 2014 homicide numbers as an approximation of 2015's, those 662 white and Hispanic victims of police shootings would make up 12% of all white and Hispanic homicide deaths. That is three times the proportion of black deaths that result from police shootings."

The Myths of Black Lives Matter
wsj.com

A Washington State University study [98] found that police were quicker to use deadly force against armed white suspects than black ones — greater scrutiny and repercussions exist with shooting blacks. It's an open secret amongst white cops patrolling

---

black neighborhoods that they can't even point their flashlights at black suspects without fear of departmental punishment, or accusations of racism. In fact, a Seattle police officer was suspended for telling a black suspect — who cops were chasing down a Seattle alleyway, *"You're gonna get your ass shot, boy!"* And the suspension is not even the crazy part. The craziness lies with the fact that the cop never said it to the fleeing suspect, it was said while in pursuit of the fleeing suspect, and the audio was captured by the cruiser's dash cam. The suspect was running on foot while the cop pursued him in the vehicle. Additionally, he wasn't suspended for mentioning shooting the suspect; the suspension was for saying "boy." Again, the suspect never heard any of this. It only came to light after Seattle police released the dash cam video following a public disclosure request and 'in the interests of fostering better police transparency'. The officer violated Seattle police department's *"bias-free policing policy."* If only the perp were white, I bet that the cop wouldn't have been suspended. Score another point for the RGI.

'You're gonna get your ass shot, boy!' Seattle police officer is suspended after shouting slur at black suspect
dailymail.co.uk

Zachary Hammond

Tori Morton, a 23-year-old female who was on her first date with 19-year-old Zachary Hammond, used Hammond's cell phone to text someone she was trying to sell drugs to, but inadvertently texted a state trooper with a similar phone number. The state trooper contacted Seneca police, who sent an undercover police officer to meet with Morton and Hammond.

At around 8:20 p.m. on July 26, 2015, Hammond, with Morton as his passenger, drove his 2001 Honda Civic through a parking lot of a Hardee's restaurant, where Morton texted the undercover officer — *"i think im beside u lol."* Lieutenant Mark Tiller was sent as backup for the undercover officer. When Lieutenant Tiller arrived, he pulled his vehicle behind Hammond's car — to block any attempted escape. Tiller then approached Hammond's car, ordering him to show his hands. Hammond did not show his hands and began to drive away from the scene. Tiller attempted to stop the driver by stepping into the path of the fleeing vehicle, but Hammond continued to accelerate and was clear of the officer. Tiller then fired two rounds from his .45 caliber handgun at close range through the open driver's side window of Hammond's car as Hammond tried to flee. Bullets struck Hammond in the left chest and left rear shoulder. The police report stated that Tiller feared being run over by Hammond's vehicle when he backed it up and then pulled forward towards the officer. Hammond was under the influence of cocaine at the time of his death.

Following the shooting, Hammond's passenger was issued a summons for possession of 10 grams (0.35 oz) of marijuana. Police allege that she had planned to sell it to an undercover officer who had set up the deal.

Seneca police Chief John Covington initially refused to release Tiller's name in violation of South Carolina's "Sunshine Law" but did finally release it twelve days after the shooting in response to the *Freedom of Information* requests. Covington referred to Tiller as a *"victim"* of *"attempted murder"* in an incident report, and stated that Tiller fired his weapon in self-defense because Hammond *"drove his vehicle directly at the officer."*

Hammond's family criticized the media for their "hypocrisy" for treating his death differently than similar police officer shootings of unarmed citizens such as Walter Scott and Samuel DuBose.

Lieutenant Mark Tiller did not face criminal charges, and the Department of Justice reviewed the case for potential federal charges, but none was expected.

Zachary Hammond shooting: officer who killed teen avoids criminal charges
theguardian.com

After the dashcam's footage was released, the White Lives Matter movement protested in full force

Black Cops

As previously noted, the hardships faced by police officers patrolling inner cities are innumerable; especially in *hoods* that are physically controlled by *hoods* and psychologically controlled by the victim*hood* mentality. Essentially, such tours are three *hoods* at once. And since the police presence is constant, the black residents typically view cops as antagonists; but no cops are viewed more antagonistically than black cops are. Black cops really face unique challenges. The perception is that they've traded black for blue, and blue ultimately serves white interests. In other words, black cops have abandoned their race to enforce institutionalized racism. Alternatively, black residents expect black cops to enforce justice for "just-us" (blacks) while practicing the color of law against those who don't share the same color of skin. Moreover, black criminals expect black cops to treat them like political prisoners. If not, they're sell-outs.

During the Ferguson fiasco of 2014, Yahoo.com reported that black cops (by all accounts) received the worst verbal abuse from protesters. Sgt. Harry Dilworth, Ferguson's most senior black officer, and 24-year Army veteran with tours in Iraq and Afghanistan discussed some of the vitriol experienced from the BLM mob:

"My God," said Dilworth, "threatening your families, getting very specific on what they were going to do to your daughter and your wife. If you have a unique name, they can Google it, go to records, and find out [personal information]."

What it's like to be a black cop in Ferguson
yahoo.com

In 1993, hip-hop artist KRS-One released a popular anti-black cop song called "Black Cop," and its lyrics still resonate in many black communities.

Here's what the West and the East have in common
Both have black cops in cars profilin'
Hardcore kids in the West got stress
In the East we are chased by the same black beast

The black cop is the only real obstacle
Black slave turned black cop is not logical
But very psychological, haven't you heard?
It's the black cop killin' black kids in Johannesburg

Whassup black cop, yo, whassup?
Your authorization says shoot your nation
You wanna uphold the law, what could you do to me?
The same law dissed the whole black community

You can't play both sides of the fence
1993 mad kids are gettin' tense

(Chorus) Black cop, black cop, black cop, black cop
Stop shootin' black people we all gonna drop
You don't even get, paid a whole lot
Take your four-five and you put it 'pon lock!
Take your M-60 and put it 'pon lock!
Take your Uzi, put it 'pon lock!
Black cop black cop black cop
Black cop black cop black cop

"Training Day" vs. "Family Matters"... In urban America, only one of these cops "Keeps it real"

Black Anti-RGI Cop

NYPD Officer Randolph Holder, a third-generation cop, responded to a call of gunfire between two rival gangs in East Harlem. When officers arrived, the two groups of urban terrorists scattered. One of the fleeing thugs robbed a bicyclist at gunpoint, led cops on a chase, and shot at them while being pursued — striking Officer Randolph in the forehead. Sadly, the five-year veteran later died at the hospital. The gunman was also wounded during the exchange but not fatally. He was apprehended and charged.

In life, Officer Holder ran towards danger, but in death, he avoided danger posed by the RGI. This fact became evident when rumors surfaced that Shakedown Sharpton was inexplicably asked by the slain officer's father to deliver the eulogy. Officer Holder's fiancée was puzzled by that idea remarking, *"He [Officer Holder] didn't like [Sharpton]. He wasn't a fan. So I don't know why [Sharpton] is speaking."* Thankfully, circus master Sharpton didn't speak at the funeral and Officer Holder was allowed to rest in peace.

Officer Holder died honoring the Hippocratic Oath

He didn't like Sharpton: Slain cop's fiancée slams possible eulogy by Rev.
nypost.com

Chapter VII

#AllLivesMatter

"Injustice anywhere is a threat to justice everywhere." – MLK

In the finite amount of time that nature allows us, I am a firm believer that all lives matter, even the lives of urban terrorists — well... admittedly, urban terrorists' lives don't really matter to me, but they undeniably matter to the prison and funeral industries. The thought/word police have interpreted the #AllLivesMatter declaration as a cheap rebuttal and dismissal to #BlackLivesMatter. In fact, the #AllLivesMatter assertion is tantamount to fighting words at BLM rallies or political events.

Martin O'Malley, a former Maryland governor, and Democratic presidential candidate, actually apologized for saying *"All lives matter"* while discussing police violence against blacks at a liberal conference in Phoenix. CNN reported:

"Several dozen demonstrators interrupted the former Maryland governor while he was speaking here at the Netroots Nation conference, a gathering of liberal activists, demanding that he address criminal justice and police brutality. When they shouted, "Black lives matter!" a rallying cry of protests that broke out after several black Americans were killed at the hands of police in recent months, O'Malley responded: "Black lives matter. White lives matter. All lives matter." The demonstrators, who were mostly black, responded by booing him and shouting him down.

O'Malley apologizes for saying 'all lives matter' at liberal conference
cnn.com

Writing on the walls, dry-erase message boards, or chalkboards is a Facebook tradition that employees have at their disposal like their virtual Facebook wall. However, Facebook's CEO, Mark Zuckerberg, had a billionaire's breakdown after #BlackLivesMatter was repeatedly crossed out on the company's walls and replaced with #AllLivesMatter.

"There have been several recent instances of people crossing out 'black lives matter' and writing 'all lives matter' on the walls" Zuckerberg wrote. "Despite my clear communication at Q&A last week that this was unacceptable, and messages from several other leaders from across the company, this has happened again. I was already very disappointed by

this disrespectful behavior before, but after my communication I now consider this malicious as well."

Mark Zuckerberg asks employees to stop crossing out 'Black Lives Matter' on the walls at Facebook's headquarters
businessinsider.com

Mark Zuckerberg
18 hrs.

There have been several recent instances of people crossing out "black lives matter" and writing "all lives matter" on the walls at MPK.

Despite my clear communication at Q&A last week that this was unacceptable, and messages from several other leaders from across the company, this has happened again. I was already very disappointed by this disrespectful behavior before, but after my communication I now consider this malicious as well.

There are specific issues affecting the black community in the United States, coming from a history of oppression and racism. 'Black lives matter' doesn't mean other lives don't -- it's simply asking that the black community also achieves the justice they deserve.

We've never had rules around what people can write on our walls -- we expect everybody to treat each other with respect. Regardless of the content or location, crossing out something means silencing speech, or that one person's speech is more important than another's. Facebook should be a service and a community where everyone is treated with respect.

This has been a deeply hurtful and tiresome experience for the black community and really the entire Facebook community, and we are now investigating the current incidents.

I hope and encourage people to participate in the Black@ town hall on 3/4 to educate themselves about what the Black Lives Matter movement is about.

👍 Like   💬 Comment   ➤ Share

Blacks make up 2 percent of Facebook's staff

The #AllLivesMatter declaration qualifies all lives, even the lives that BLM claims it's representing, and the lives it neglects. Neglected lives such as that of Zaevion Dobson, a fifteen-year-old hero who was killed when he shielded three girls from urban terrorists' gunfire. The super predators fired upon a group of school kids celebrating the holiday. Zaevion saved those girls from imminent danger because #AllLivesMatter. Tragically, only four months later, urban terrorism would again visit Zaevion Dobson's family. This time, the urban Grim Reapers snatched the life of his younger cousin, twelve-year-old Jajuan Latham. The preteen was struck in the head during a drive-by shooting while sitting in the back seat of his father's parked vehicle at a park gathering. His murder suspiciously occurred just hours after attending a "Stop the Violence" celebrity basketball game held in Zaevion Dobson's honor. Needless to say, neither cousin qualified for the #BlackLivesMatter hashtag.

Zavion sacrificed himself while Jajuan was sacrificed by the community's apathy towards urban terrorism

Hero football player's family opens up about his sacrifice
cbsnews.com

12-year-old boy killed in Knoxville gang shooting
wate.com

The indisputable fact is that one of these hashtags is exclusive whereas the other is inclusive; one of them exists to *"protest"* while the other exists to *"protect."* The life of five-year-old Layla Peterson, who was shot and killed while sitting on her grandfather's lap, most certainly matters! The life of six-year-old Logan Lipton, who was stabbed to death in his bed during a home invasion, most certainly matters! The life of fifty-one-year-old Robert Barnes — a homeless veteran beaten to death (over a lie) by an angry mob of adults and juveniles — most certainly matters! Yet, only one of these hashtags honors the memory of these types of innocent victims. #AllLivesMatter ensures that victims who would have otherwise been hashtag anonymous, receive the love and honor that they deserve. Super Bowl commercials are more memorable to most people than these tragic stories. But #AllLivesMatter can change that gloomy reality.

  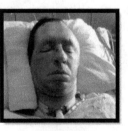

Layla Peterson   Logan Lipton   Robert Barnes

In summation, this super short chapter is simply saying that #AllLivesMatter doesn't diminish the #BlackLivesMatter creed. Even so, #BlackLivesMatter isn't a bridge to racial harmony; it's a bridge to nowhere that should be burned.

More blameless victims of super predators
#AllLivesMatter > BlackLivesMatter

Chapter VIII

Land of the Free, Home of the Offended

"It's the government's job to protect a lot of things, but your feelings ain't one of them." – Bill Maher

Oh, my beloved America, what are you becoming? Many say that America doesn't have an official religion; I vehemently disagree! Presently, our seemingly state-sponsored religion is political correctness and anyone who doesn't kneel before it will be publicly sacrificed. Eventually, there will be no need to fill in religious denomination on birth certificates; "political correctness" will already be pre-stamped. The gods of PC are ensuring that America has one foot in the grave and the other on a banana peel — which is why I have a vendetta against political correctness and the thought/word police; they undesirably affect my life. I'm not talking about traditional police who *protect and serve*; I'm talking about the thought/word police who want us to *prostrate and serve.* The former are easily identifiable from their blue uniforms, while the latter are difficult to identify because they dress as civilians, and use political correctness as their billy club. Additionally, the regular police enforce laws whereas the thought/word police enforce PC ideologies. I agree with Edward Bernays' assessment of today's America: *"The United States has become a small room where a single whisper is magnified thousands of times[99]."*

Just as fire can't burn without oxygen, the RGI couldn't effectively exist without this climate of political correctness. Today's unchecked PC has shaped and sustained this current atmosphere where any criticism of the RGI is construed as racist. Consequently, the RGI has been free to impose its divisive agenda without significant pushback; inevitably causing race-relations to decay.

In 1992, Barbara Jordan, the first black woman from a southern state elected to the House of Representatives, used her keynote speech at the Democratic National Convention to warn her liberal base about political correctness:

"We are one, we Americans. We're one and we reject any intruder who seeks to divide us on the basis of race and color. We honor cultural identity. We always have; we always will. But separatism is not allowed. Separatism is not the American way. We must not allow ideas like political correctness to divide us and cause us to reverse hard-won achievements in human rights and civil rights."

I wish that my high school had offered classes on political correctness to compliment the political science classes. That way, I could've failed political correctness in school and moved on with my life, instead of repeatedly failing political correctness in the real world. Understandably, sometimes the best things said are the things left unsaid. However, political correctness is a straightjacket. Whenever reality conflicts with ideology, reality must be restrained — even marginally disagreeable actions, words, or thoughts, are now considered colossal violations. In a society that values and honors freedom of speech and expression, we've allowed this counter-culture phenomenon to fester and grow.

College Campuses

Nowhere is PC more evident and alive than on college campuses. From being a place where Critical Race Theory (CRT), which teaches that racism is engrained in the fabric and system of the American society, is being propagated, to being the home of free speech zones, safe zones, speech codes, and other micromanaged forms of censorship. Today's campuses are incubators for victimology, and in these places of so-called "higher learning," students are essentially radicalized by political correctness. According to a 2010 study conducted by the Association of American Colleges and Universities, only 30 percent of college seniors strongly agreed with the question: *"Is it safe to hold unpopular opinions on campus[100]?"* Moreover, the study found that the students' confidence to safely hold unpopular opinions declined from freshman to senior year. In the column *"The Coddling of the American Mind,"* written for The Atlantic *(09/15)*, Greg Lukianoff and Jonathan Haidt revealed:

"Two terms have risen quickly from obscurity into common campus parlance. Microaggressions are small actions or word choices that seem on

their face to have no malicious intent but that are thought of as a kind of violence nonetheless. For example, by some campus guidelines, it is a microaggression to ask an Asian American or Latino American "Where were you born?," because this implies that he or she is not a real American. Trigger warnings are alerts that professors are expected to issue if something in a course might cause a strong emotional response. For example, some students have called for warnings that Chinua Achebe's 'Things Fall Apart' describes racial violence and that F. Scott Fitzgerald's 'The Great Gatsby' portrays misogyny and physical abuse, so that students who have been previously victimized by racism or domestic violence can choose to avoid these works, which they believe might "trigger" a recurrence of past trauma."

An analysis by the Institute of Medicine[101] has found that "trigger warnings" aren't much help in actually overcoming trauma — the best approach is controlled exposure to it — and experts say avoidance can reinforce suffering. That's easier said than done. Political correctness has such a strong chokehold on many colleges that several popular comediennes refuse to tour them. Comedienne Chris Rock explained to Vulture magazine[102]:

"I stopped playing colleges, and the reason is because they're way too conservative... Not in their political views — not like they're voting Republican — but in their social views and their willingness not to offend anybody. Kids raised on a culture of 'We're not going to keep score in the game because we don't want anybody to lose.' Or just ignoring race to a fault."

Jerry Seinfeld Says Colleges Are Too Politically Correct, Kids Don't Understand Racism Or Sexism
huffingtonpost.com

[Author's Note: Comedy is the final frontier for free speech. So, it's very telling that legendary comedians had second thoughts about performing on the college circuit.]

Frankenstein Attacks Liberal Bastion

Political correctness is destined to self-destruct, but ultimately, liberals will have to be the ones to destroy this monster it has created. As more PC-radicalized students turn against their administrators, professors, or universities for micro-aggressions, liberals will have no choice but to take a stand. As evidenced by a number of race-based protests that afflicted college campuses nationwide, — including Missouri University, where professional protesters were bused in by BLM, the football team went on strike, a poop swastika was alleged, and both president and chancellor resigned — the most frequent victims of political correctness are liberals. And uber-liberal Oberlin College provides an important case study of the PC monster turning on its creator/enabler.

Oberlin College, located in Oberlin, Ohio, is celebrated for being the first American institution of higher learning to regularly admit female and black students in addition to white males. According to Oberlin's website, it has approximately 2,900 students. Among them, twenty-percent are students of color. Despite Oberlin's historical commitments to black students long before it became fashionable, a black student union, named *"Abusua,"* the Ghanian word for *"clan,"* felt that Oberlin hasn't done enough for black students lately. As a result, the group addressed a fourteen-page manifesto of fifty "non-negotiable" demands to the Trustees, President, and other senior administrators, accompanied by a roll of student signatures. The list of demands was hand-delivered to the offices of the President, Vice-President, and Dean of Students.

The Demands

The opening paragraph of the demands, read as if was an excerpt from the *"Twelve Years a Slave"* movie. Blacks weren't even this demanding when they were first admitted to the school in the 1800's.

"Oberlin College and Conservatory is an unethical institution. From capitalizing on massive labor exploitation across campus, to the Conservatory of Music treating Black and other students of color as less than through its everyday running, Oberlin College unapologetically acts as unethical institution, antithetical to its historical vision. In the 1830s, this school claimed a legacy of supporting its Black students. However, that legacy has amounted to nothing more than a public relations campaign initiated to benefit the image of the institution and not the Africana people it was set out for. Along the same lines stated by UNC Chapel Hill students in their 2015 document "A Collective Response to AntiBlackness," you include Black and other students of color in the institution and mark them with the words "equity, inclusion and diversity," when in fact this institution functions on the premises of imperialism, white supremacy, capitalism, ableism, and a cissexist heteropatriarchy. Oberlin College and Conservatory uses the limited number of Black and Brown students to color in its brochures, but then erases us from student life on this campus. You profit off of our accomplishments and invisible labor, yet You expect us to produce personal solutions to institutional incompetencies. We as a College defined "high risk," "low income," "disadvantaged" community should not have to carry the burden of deconstructing the white supremacist, patriarchal, capitalist system that we took no part in creating, yet is so deeply embedded in the soil upon which this institution was built."

The Abusua document also emphasized, *"These are demands and not suggestions,"* and *"If these demands are not taken seriously, immediate action from the Africana community will follow."* Just as BLM never has die-ins, #BlackBrunch, protest etc. where they're needed, this grievance group's demands aren't even demanded at HBCUs (Historically Black Colleges and Universities).

Abusua's six main goals for Oberlin to accommodate included:

• *A four percent annual increase in enrollment of students of color from each of the Americas, the Caribbean, and continent of Africa from 2016 to 2022.*
• *An increase in black administrators and faculty members across departments and governing bodies.*
• *The divestment from all prisons and Israel.*
• *Exclusive safe spaces for black students with designated rooms at Wilder Hall, the Science Center, and Mudd Library.*
• *Elimination of "institutional complacency" that allows violence against black students.*
• *The "eradication of hegemony" in curriculum.*

The student union also alleges that its demands have been raised before and were ignored.

"This was never acceptable and will not longer be tolerated," it read. "As you will see, these are not polite requests but concrete and unmalleable demands. Failure to meet them will result in a full and forceful response from the community you fail to support."

Among the other demands were:

• *Renaming of four <u>academic</u> buildings to honor Wendell Logan, who created the jazz department; Avery Brooks, a world renowned actor best known for portraying Capt. Benjamin Sisko on "Star Trek: Deep Space Nine"; professor Yakubu Saaka and professor emeritus Booker Peek; and sculptor Edmonia Lewis, "as an acknowledgement of the debt owed to her for the violence that she experienced at this institution."*
• *More transparency in the faculty recruitment process for the jazz department, and in the admissions and retention efforts of the college in general.*
• *A six percent annual increase in grant offers versus loan offers for black students for the next five years.*
• *An increase in funding for internships and career opportunities for all black students.*

- *An $8.20 per hour stipend for black student leaders' continuous organizing efforts.*
- *The firing and promotion of certain professors and staff.*
- *That black prospective students be interviewed by admissions officers trained in race consciousness practices.*
- *Free housing for black international students unable to return to their home countries during post-semester breaks.*
- *An online database outlining deadlines, dates, and forms critical for the successful academic journey of black students.*
- *Financial aid workshops for black students by black financial aid officers.*
- *Funding for an event for black first-year students during orientation week.*
- *Institutional and financial support for a black bridge program between the Oberlin public school system and Oberlin College.*
- *A bridge program for recently released prisoners of the Grafton Correctional Institution to enroll at Oberlin College.*
- *An "Intro to the Black Experience" course for all students as a graduation requirement.*
- *Elimination of graduation requirements for Western and classical-centered courses; or required equivalent courses in African Diaspora.*
- *Creation of a department focusing on languages of Africana peoples, including Kiswahili, Yoruba, Menda, Xhosa, Creole, Black English, Jamaican Patois, and more.*
- *Health care and insurance through the college as benefits for all employees.*
- *A meal every work shift for workers at college dining hall services.*
- *Rehiring of community members terminated from jobs at the Oberlin Inn before its renovation.*
- *Discontinuation of the "no trespass list," which Abusua says disproportionately targets black people.*
- *A free busing system for Oberlin public school students, paid for by the college.*
- *A program allowing community members to take one free course per semester at the college.*
- *Establishment of a payment in lieu of taxes program by the college, to be approved by the city.*

Undoubtedly, this level of victimology is rooted in Oberlin's curriculum. If more proof is needed about Oberlin's liberalism, note that actress Lena Durham is an alumnus. These students have been emboldened and coddled, instead of being pushed and challenged. Thus, the entitlement mentality has gone rogue. Now, these apprentices of aggrievements don't want equal rights; they want special rights, arguably superior rights! The arrogance to submit a "non-negotiable" list of demands to an entity that

---

TALEEB STARKES

already practices appeasement as an outreach mechanism signifies that political correctness is reaching a point of no return. Demanding that prisoners are enrolled, staff fired, and shared governance, really shows how far the rabbit hole goes.

'Unethical' Oberlin College handed 50 demands by black student union
theoberlinnewstribune.com

In the 1830s, Oberlin was the only college to admit black students, and today is probably the only non-HBCU where there are 15 officially recognized black student organizations — twice the amount of student organizations dedicated to Asian/Pacific Islander, Latino/Latina, Jewish, and Native American students COMBINED. Remember, black students, are a minority of Oberlin's student populace yet...

1. ***Abusua*** (the Ghanian word for 'Clan') is a Black student organization that strives to promote a sense of community for Black students on the Oberlin campus. Political activism and cultural unity are emphasized through various social and cultural events and programs throughout the school year which include communications, social and cultural activities, academic affairs and publications. All Black students are encouraged to participate in the various facets of Abusua.

2. ***The African Students Association's (ASA)*** purposes include the following: to enhance and sustain unity among Africans in Oberlin, to coordinate African students' campus activities, and to act as a coalition-builder with other campus organizations; to join and actively participate in the National African Students' Association, to identify and promote African cultures, and to encourage participation in the development and affairs of the African continent. ASA also strives to provide a network for prospective African students abroad and at home, as a means of enhancing education, to communicate and cooperate with other organizations of the African Diaspora, and to approach colleges, universities and scholarship foundations for merit scholarships for African students.

3. ***Agape Fellowship*** is a Bible study group that provides a place for Christian students and especially for African-American students to study the Bible and to fellowship. Agape Fellowship also provides a place for non-Christian students seeking a better understanding of the Bible and Christianity.

4. ***And What!?*** is a Hip Hop dance troupe that focuses on performance and the elements of Hip Hop cultural education, Emceeing, Deejaying, Breakdancing, and Graffiti Art.

5. **Dance Diaspora** is a student dance company focused on dance performance of the Black experience around the world.

6. **Eclipse** is a photo-journal yearbook cataloging people and moments from the Africana community.

7. **Essence** is a dance class to develop creativity in performance through modern dance, Afro-forms, and Black vernacular dance.

8. **In Solidarity** is a collaborative publication by People of Color at Oberlin-distributed twice a month to report and analyze important events across our communities from the campus to a global level.

9. **Nommo**, Swahili for "the word," is an Africana student literary and news publication. Contributors to Nommo include students, staff, faculty, and alumni. Nommo explores relevant issues in the Africana community through poetry, prose, interviews, visual art, and essays.

10. **OBSSO** coordinates and encourages study tables and groups to share support and mechanisms for success among Black natural science students. OBSSO also gathers and disseminations information regarding science and health opportunities for Black students.

11. **OCMBMG** creates a base of academic, social, musical, and cultural support and guidance for Oberlin Conservatory's Black students.

12. **MSA** provides support for and promotes an educational framework for Muslim students at Oberlin from the U.S. and abroad. This framework provides support for religious, cultural, and educational activities including religious observances, festivals and speakers at Oberlin. MSA also explores and expresses the changing diversity of the Muslim world today.

13. **SOCA** is an organization in which students from the Caribbean unite to celebrate and honor their ancestry through educational and social events for the campus and community.

14. **Sisters of the Yam** is a discussion and support group for Black women at Oberlin College.

15. **VFC** nurtures the needs of students and community members who seek to worship Christ through Black American gospel and spiritual songs. Members of VFC promote the joy and message of Jesus through music and fellowship.

Black student group expressing "tolerance" at Dartmouth University's library

This asinine list of demands shows how the black student grievance groups claim not to want blacks treated differently, but then turn around and want blacks to be treated differently via race-based groups and set-asides. Only politicians talk from both sides of their mouths more. There are even more black-centered organizations outside of college that specifically contain the world black, but don't want blacks to be viewed race first. Here's a quick "black" list:

- American Association of **Blacks** in Energy
- The Association of **Black** Psychologists
- National Association of **Black** Accountants
- National Association of **Black** Hotel Owners, Operators, and Developers
- National Association of **Black** Journalists
- National **Black** Business Council
- National **Black** Chamber of Commerce
- National **Black** MBA Association
- National **Black** Nurses Association
- National Coalition of 100 **Black** Women
- National Society of **Black** Engineers
- Organization of **Black** Designers
- National Organization of **Black** Law Enforcement Executives (NOBLE)
- 100 **Black** Men of America
- The **Black** Clergy
- The **Black** Clergy Women
- Congressional **Black** Caucus

Countless other "black" entities and organizations exist such as the NAACP, National Council of Negro Women, National Urban League, United Negro College Fund, etc., that don't overtly have the word "black" in their names, but their missions are unquestionably race-specific.

Dr. Frankenstein Says No

A simple, two-lettered word caused devastating damage to Oberlin's black student group. And to the group's detriment, there's a strong possibility that the word may even be used again in any setting that they attempt to take hostage. The unassertive but yet assertive word is "no." In a move that liberal colleges may cite as dangerous, Oberlin's president, Marvin Krislov did something unprecedented, he responded to the list of demands without placating. *"Some of the solutions it proposes are deeply troubling,"* Krislov wrote in a response posted on Oberlin's website. *"I will not respond directly to any document that explicitly rejects the notion of collaborative engagement. Many of its demands contravene principles of shared governance. And it contains personal attacks on a number of faculty and staff members who are dedicated and valued members of this community."*

Oberlin president says no to black students' demands
pbs.org

"Safe Spaces"

On May 17, 1954, the Supreme Court of the United States handed down its decision regarding the case called Brown v. Board of Education of Topeka, Kansas, — in which the plaintiffs charged that the education of black children in separate public schools from their white counterparts was unconstitutional. Brown v. Board of Education meant that the University of Alabama had to be desegregated. In January of 1963, following his election as Governor of Alabama, George Wallace famously stated in his inaugural address, *"Segregation now, segregation tomorrow, segregation forever."*

When black students Vivian Malone and James A. Hood showed up at the University of Alabama campus in Tuscaloosa to enroll on June 11, 1963, the governor demonstrated his devotion to segregation. In what historians often refer to as the "Stand in the Schoolhouse Door," the governor literally stood in the doorway as federal authorities tried to allow the students to enter. When he refused to budge, President John F. Kennedy called for one hundred troops from the Alabama National Guard to assist federal officials. Governor Wallace chose to step aside rather than incite violence. The rest is history.

Gov. Wallace would be proud of today's climate

Will the history books of tomorrow remember today's period of millennial blacks calling for segregation under the guise of "safe spaces" on college campuses, even after prior generations zealously fought to end segregation? The contradiction of denouncing Jim Crow history while simultaneously petitioning for segregation isn't lost upon black grievance groups. They don't mind turning back the clock, as long as the hand that's doing the turning is black. In other words, diversity and separation are only acceptable if they're the ones diversifying and separating. Separate place + separate rules = equal treatment?

In today's PC era, only one of these signs is racist

College is supposed to be a "safe space" *for* ideas, not *from* ideas. Besides, blacks already have race-based "safe spaces"; they're called HBCUs (Historically Black Colleges and Universities). It's laughable that these BLM college groups bitch about trigger words, while n-words with triggers are terrorizing urban America.

College Campuses Call For 'Safe Spaces'
npr.org

The inner cities sure could use some safe spaces for children to play, and elders to relax, without fear of becoming collateral damage. But those disingenuous black students' groups would never take this fight to the places where it truly belongs. Regina Banks, a Baltimore mother, told *The Baltimore Sun* that she refuses to send her children to the playground just across the street. It's dangerous and littered with drug vials, used condoms, and liquor bottles. Instead, she uses the front porch next door as a "safe haven" and play space for her children and their friends. *"We're across from a playground. However, we had to make our own playground,"* Banks said. *"I'm a mom. It's scary[103]."*

Language Barrier

Controlling the language is also a key component of these budding authoritarians. During the Baltimore tsunami of 2015, we've learned thug is a code word for nigger[104]. We have gotten to a point where people can't even be judged by the content of their character. Calling a thug a thug is now taboo even though calling cancer by any other name doesn't make it less cancerous. The Guardian, a liberal British newspaper, implied that correcting people's grammar is racist. *"The people pointing out the mistakes are more likely to be older, wealthier, whiter, or just plain academic than the people they're treating with condescension[105],"* opined Mona Chalabi, The Guardian's data editor. Yep, the grammar police are racist. In Seattle, officials no longer use "brown bag" in official documents and discussions because it's potentially offensive[106]. The Department of Education has banned references to "dinosaurs," "birthdays," "Halloween" and dozens of other words on city-issued tests because they fear such words "could evoke unpleasant emotions in the students[107]." Dinosaurs, for example, call to mind evolution, which might upset fundamentalists and Halloween suggests paganism. The

University of New Hampshire once offered a Bias-Free Language Guide[108] that — according to the university's website — was *"meant to invite inclusive excellence in [the] campus community."*

Problematic Word	Inclusive Substitute
Rich	Person of material wealth
Poor	Person who lacks advantages that others have; low economic status related to a person's education, occupation, and income
Elders	Senior Citizens
Handicapped or Physically-challenged	Non-Disabled
Caucasian	European-American individual
Illegal Alien	Person seeking asylum, Undocumented Immigrant, Refugee
American	U.S. Citizen or Resident of the U.S.
Foreigners	International People

University of Minnesota

Armed with the thought/word-police's billy club, the University of Minnesota's Black Student Union wanted the college to censor race from its crime alerts. The BSU wanted the alerts to be politically-correct instead of simply being correct. If the BSU had its way, the crime alerts would generically read like this:

"A homo sapien has allegedly committed a crime on or near the university... Vigilance is advised."

It would also be accompanied by an apology that expressed deep sorrow to any homo sapien offended by its posting. Fortunately, the university's crime alerts are written by the University of Minnesota Police Department (UMPD), emailed to students, faculty, and staff — plus posted on its UMPD webpage. The UMPD's web page explains that the alerts simply highlight "crimes that may pose an ongoing threat to the University community." However, the BSU selfishly prefers that campus sensibilities be emphasized over campus safety because the crime alerts routinely contained high amounts of melanin. In other words, black suspects dominated the alerts.

Determined to change this lopsided dynamic, the Black Student Union formulated a remedy. Unfortunately, their remedy wasn't to address the unrelenting black crime, such as robberies, which had increased twenty-seven percent on and around the campus. Instead, their solution was to merge with other Black-identifying groups and petition the university to remove race from crime alerts.

'U' Students Want Crime Alerts To Avoid Using Racial Descriptions
minnesota.cbslocal.com

The petition was issued by members of the African American and African Studies, Black Faculty and Staff Association, Black Graduate, and Professional Student Association, Black Men's Forum, Black Student Union, and Huntley House for African American Males. The organizations wrote that while campus safety is crucial, the profiling could be devastating for black male students.

"[We] unanimously agree that campus safety should be of the UMPD's utmost importance; however, efforts to reduce crime should never be at the expense of our Black men, or any specific group of people likely to be targeted. In addition to causing Black men to feel unsafe and distrusted, racial profiling is proven to inflict negative psychological effects on its victims."

Besides being the first and only race to ever request that the university race-censor its crime alerts, these black organizations evidently have no issue with emphasizing race to identify their respective groups (as previously noted); yet, race is taboo when identifying black criminals. The irony and hypocrisy would be comical if it weren't true.

The president of the Black Men's Forum said that members of his organization feel threatened whenever racial descriptions are provided in crime alerts. Again, the black criminals created this reality, not the university. These black grievance organizations characteristically mislabel criminal profiling as racial profiling.

Admittedly, I'm no social engineer. But, in three words, I'm going to provide some ingenious advice that if heeded, would prevent a certain group from being disproportionately mentioned on campus crime alerts, and even nationwide police reports.

DON'T.... COMMIT... CRIMES!!!

Coincidentally, these three words can also be used to reverse any overrepresentation in prisons.

The grievance letter also contained twelve recommendations for the UMPD, including mandatory diversity training for officers.

The Vice President of University Services, Pamela Wheelock, responded to the grievance letter and utilized common sense to end the discourse. Naturally, the black organizations and PC gods were disappointed with her for logic of placing campus safety over political correctness. She concluded:

"I firmly believe that a well-informed community is an asset to public safety...I believe that sharing more information in our Crime Alerts, not less, is most beneficial in terms of public safety, especially when that information is available. The information we share can include a complete description of suspects, unique identifying characteristics such as an accent or a distinctive piece of clothing, or the description of vehicles involved. We have reviewed what other Big Ten Universities and local colleges and universities include, and our practice of including the race of a suspect when it is available from a victim's description is consistent with their practices."

Although the University of Minnesota maintained its rational position on race-censorship, the black organizations can still enjoy the fact that the mainstream media often censor race.

Trickle-Down Effect

Sadly, these aggrieved college students are our future leaders. And following in their shadows are impressionable high schoolers, who will likely inherit their grievances without a second thought. In fact, a high school in Oak Park, Illinois, exemplifies how the wheels on the grievance bus go round-and-round.

Nathaniel Rouse, a seven-year principal of majority-white Oak Park and River Forest high school, said he had been approached by black students in the building who tried to make sense of the grand jury's decision not to prosecute police officer Darren Wilson for shooting Michael Brown in Ferguson, Mo. Therefore, in the spirit of his school district's five-year strategic plan, which has a running theme of racial equity, Principal Rouse, who is black, decided to host a Black Lives Matter event.

The event, tactically held during Black History Month, was supposed to ignite a constructive dialogue about race, but instead sparked an entirely different race discussion from white parents after white students were denied entry to the event. It was limited to only black students. According to the school's website, its student population was 55 percent white, 27 percent black, nine percent Hispanic, six percent multiracial, and three percent Asian.

It's a melting pot. So naturally, white parents were offended that a school/community that prides itself on diversity and inclusion would exclude white students who wanted to attend. Principal Rouse replied that exclusivity wasn't the intent. He said the decision to allow only black students was based on an idea known as "affinity grouping," the philosophy that students of one racial persuasion are able to express themselves fully and safely.

"In order for us to move forward, I believe the affinity group is the safe way for us to move forward in a safe environment," he said. *"I found it has been far easier for me to talk about my experiences with racism with individuals that look like me. I still struggle myself with talking about my experiences with people who don't look like me,"* he lamented.

This event was promoted as a dialogue about race relations but in actuality was a monologue on victimhood, justified by the latest PC term "affinity grouping." Perhaps affinity grouping is what Jim Crow was all along. I wonder how the principal explained to the students that the event focused on discrimination when the event itself was discriminatory. With a wink and smile, he probably explained that it was "payback."

OPRF parents upset 'Black Lives Matter' assembly excludes other races
chicagotribune.com

Handy, Dandy, Race Card

Monopoly, the timeless and beloved board game, has a highly valued *"Get out of Jail Free"* card that can be used at a player's discretion. The coveted card can only be used by the player who possesses it. In colleges where blacks are a minority, black students carry a similar card that can be used at their discretion: the race card. And, it seemingly has limitless equity that black students can use ad nauseam — even when examples of racism in college settings are exposed as hoaxes. These race hoaxes or, more aptly, false flag operations only persist because... black lies matter.

Yik Yak threat at SVSU said, 'I'm going to shoot every black person I can on campus'
mlive.com

Kean University

Black students at Kean University were petrified to attend classes after a series of anonymous death threats targeted them online. The threats, which included a promise to *"kill every black male and female at Kean University,"* appeared under the Twitter handle @keanuagainstblk (Kean University against black). The first threat — *"kean university twitter against blacks is for everyone who hates blacks people"* — appeared during a campus rally that was held to show solidarity with students across the nation who complained about racism at other college campuses. Then came a tweet about a bomb being on campus, and continued with tweets threatening to shoot and kill Kean's black students.

Fortunately, the racist would-be-killer was bluffing. After all, the killer had ample time to kill blacks as she marched with them. Yep, the would-be-killer was a black woman, Kayla-Simone McKelvey, a recent graduate of Kean, 2014 homecoming queen, president of the Pan African Student Union, and now, self-described race activist was charged by summons with third-degree creating a false public alarm. Police say McKelvey participated in the student rally but left midway through and walked to a computer station at the university's library. Once there, McKelvey created the anonymous Twitter account – @keanuagainstblk – and began posting threats of violence against black Kean students. After making the posts, McKelvey returned to the rally and spread awareness of the threats. That night, on her personal Twitter account, which has since been deleted, she posted photos of the rally and screenshots of the threatening tweets.

Twitter threats to black Kean students made by black alum, police say
nj.com

According to Kean's student newspaper[109], McKelvey was also the organizer of a rally based on allegations of racism against a professor and Kean's Student Organization, but that *"little to no evidence emerged to support the claims."*

Twitter dee... Twitter dumb

Missouri U

Racism just seemed to follow the president of the Missouri Student Association, and his social media kept the public pertinently informed about the ubiquitous racism at Missouri University. He once took to Facebook to vent about strangers who were riding in the rear of a pickup truck and screaming racial slurs at him. Here's the partial post about the pick-up truck incident, and in true millennial fashion, he prefaced the post with an unnecessary trigger warning.

"I just want to say how extremely hurt and disappointed I am. Last night as I walking [sic] through campus, some guys riding on the back of a pickup truck decided that it would be okay to continuously scream NIGGER at me. I really just want to know why my simple existence is such a threat to society. For those of you who wonder why I'm always talking

about the importance of inclusion and respect, it's because I've experienced moments like this multiple times at THIS [sic] university, making me not feel included here.

With its own agenda to advance, the local NAACP chapter joined the racial fright-fest by establishing a confidential telephone hotline for University of Missouri students to report racial threats.

Payton Head
September 12 · Columbia, MO ·

WARNING: EXPLICIT LANGUAGE: I just want to say how extremely hurt and disappointed I am. Last night as I walking through campus, some guys riding on the back of a pickup truck decided that it would be okay to continuously scream NIGGER at me. I really just want to know why my simple existence is such a threat to society. For those of you who wonder why I'm always talking about the importance of inclusion and respect, it's because I've experienced moments like this multiple times at THIS university, making me not feel included here. Many of you are so privileged

---

He forgot to mention that the truck had a Confederate flag painted on its hood.

And then, that phantom menace called racism found the president of Missouri Student Association again (the poor fella must have a tracking device). This time, he took to Facebook to warn his fellow black students about the looming danger. He pleaded to students to take precaution and stay away from the windows in residence halls because the KKK was sighted on campus. Fortunately for the students, he was on top of the situation. In the same message, he stated that he was working with the Missouri University Police Department (MUPD), state troopers, and National Guard on the matter. He's a true leader!

Payton Head
9 mins ·

Students please take precaution. Stay away from the windows in residence halls. The KKK has been confirmed to be sighted on campus. I'm working with the MUPD, the state trooper and the National Guard.

84 Likes · 10 Comments · 141 Shares

Sacrificing himself for the team... Right?

Well, it may have appeared as if the MSU president was on the front line for his fellows, but actually, he was launching a false flag operation. His plot was foiled when Missouri U's official alert system repudiated his claim and requested that no more rumors be disseminated.

MU Alert
@MUalert

There is no immediate threat to campus. Please do not spread rumors and follow @MUAlert at mualert.missouri.edu for updates.

11/11/15, 12:19 AM

Fraud exposed

He subsequently deleted the post about the KKK threat, issued a statement apologizing for the *"misinformation,"* and advised people to only get their information from the MU Alert system's website or Twitter page. Noticeably, the prez didn't apologize for his fallacious claim of *"working with the MUPD, the state trooper and the National Guard."*

MSA president apologizes for sharing false rumors of KKK on MU campus
krcgtv.com

University at Albany

I bet that Rosa Parks turned in her grave as news quickly spread about the three black female students at the University at Albany being physically attacked on a city bus by a group of whites who used racial epithets — all while other passengers and the driver sat silently by. The outrage on social media was instant after college student, Asha Burwell, one of the alleged victims, cried Twitter tears.

Amongst her many tweets were, *"I just got jumped on a bus while people hit us and call us the "n" word and NO ONE helped us,"* and *"I can't believe I just experienced what it's like to be beaten because of my skin color."* She also recalled how she begged people for help while being beaten, but was told to *"shut* the f*ck up." Adding insult to injury, these people were her fellow SUNY classmates, she claimed. As far as police assistance, she tweeted that *"they didn't even seem concerned."*

Asha Burwell @AshaBurwell · Jan 29
I just got jumped on a bus while people hit us and called us the "n" word and NO ONE helped us.

RETWEETS   LIKES
1,761   **731**

10:31 PM - 29 Jan 2016 · Details

Asha Burwell
@AshaBurwell

I can't believe I just experienced what it's like to be beaten because of the color of my skin.

RETWEETS   LIKES
1,083   426

7:08 AM - 30 Jan 2016

Asha Burwell @AshaBurwell · Jan 30
I begged for people to help us and instead of help they told us to "shut he f*ck up" and continuously hit us in the head

Asha Burwell @AshaBurwell · Jan 30
Called SUNY police and they didn't even seem concerned, just transferred us to Albany police who told us they should've helped

Asha Burwell @AshaBurwell · Jan 30
And these were my fellow classmates, people that attend MY school

The outrage on social media was immediate; supporters nationwide used the hashtag *#DefendBlackGirlsUAlbany*, and a campus rally "against racism" attracted hundreds of people. At the rally, Asha Burwell declared, *"We are shocked, upset, but we will remain unbroken, we stand here with strength because we value our worth as black women and as human beings in general."* Tyreek Burwell, Asha Burwell's brother, and offensive lineman for the San Diego Chargers tweeted a threatening message to one of the wrongfully accused individuals that stated, *"just found out you were one of the dudes that put your hands on my little sister. Hope the police get to you before I do."*

Tyreek Burwell @
@TyreekBurwell

@WillBx just found out you were one of the dudes that put your hands on my little sister. Hope the police get to you before I do.

1/30/16, 3:13 AM

Disturbed by the incident, the university's black president posted an emotional letter[110] on the school's website.

"Dear Students, Faculty and Staff:

Early this morning, three of our students were harassed and assaulted while riding on a CDTA bus on Western Ave. in Albany.

The students, who are Black women, stated that racial slurs were used by the perpetrators, whom they described as a group of 10 to 12 white males and females.

I am deeply concerned, saddened and angry about this incident. There is no place in the UAlbany community for violence, no place for racial intolerance and no place for gender violence.

I am out of town today. I have decided to cut my trip short and will be returning to Albany as soon as I can to address this situation.

In the meantime, I have been in direct contact with the Provost and executive leadership team and have directed that the University respond rapidly and forcefully.

Our police, our student affairs personnel and our Office of Diversity and Inclusion staff are working together to support our young women.

We are working closely with the Albany Police Department to identify the persons responsible. If those individuals are UAlbany students, we will hold them fully accountable for their behavior.

I call upon all members of the University at Albany to unite. We must show the world that we stand for inclusiveness and stand against bias, violence and hatred.

Our annual Dr. Martin Luther King Jr. celebration will be held on the evening of Monday, Feb. 1. As we reflect on the principles and values that Dr. King stood for, let us come together in solidarity to reaffirm our values.

Now is the time to recommit to our principles of inclusivity and diversity and send a strong message that we will not tolerate bias, hatred and violence in our University."

The story even caught the attention of Hillary Clinton, who condemned the attack on Twitter saying, *"There's no excuse for racism and violence on a college campus."*

"Hot Sauce" Hillary knows that black women are the Dems' most loyal voting bloc

All the ingredients for a successful "Black Lies Matter" campaign were in effect: a white-on-black incident, usage of racial slurs, other whites refused to intervene, and the case treated as a non-issue by police. It was Tawana Brawley 2016. But surely, a story like this didn't happen in twenty-first century America, right? Exactly! In fact, the evidence stood contrary to how the so-called victims portrayed the series of events; the three individuals were not the victims of a crime, they were the perpetrators. Police said video and eyewitness accounts indicated that the women were never *"targeted in any manner due to their race,"* and the only person heard uttering racial epithets was one of the defendants. There was only one victim, a white 19-year-old female, who was actually assaulted by the three students. As a result, they were charged with third-degree assault and false filing of a police report.

SUNY Albany students who claimed racial attack will be charged for assault and false reporting
nydailynews.com

If convicted, maybe they'll receive a Presidential Pardon

Book's Conclusion

Although the RGI is sustained by its propaganda machine (the Black press/Black Twitter), legislative arm (Congressional Black Caucus), and splinter groups (such as Black Lives Matter), the three entities that actually give renewable life to the RGI are victimhood, white guilt, and political correctness. I refer to them as the "*Unholy Trinity*." And with liberalism as its ally, the RGI naively believes that it's too big to fail.

Admittedly, the RGI is a formidable opponent with many tentacles, and the quagmire it has created will remain intact for the foreseeable future. However, by aggressively confronting the RGI and its support system, its walls will eventually collapse like those of Jericho.

If we truly desire to become one nation under God, the grievance genie has to be placed back in its bottle and then sealed for eternity.

America's future is ours to create.

****Thanks for Listening****

Email: *Taleeb@theuncivilwar.info*

Twitter: *@TaleebStarkes*

Endnotes

1 "My Larger Education," published 1911 Booker T. Washington
2 "Al Sharpton's Secret Work As FBI Informant," thesmokinggun.com, 4/7/14
3 "Family Member Confirms to CNN That #BlackLivesMatter Activist Shaun King Is White," mediaite.com, 8/20/15
4 "Rachel Dolezal Announces New Book on Racial Identity," ew.com, 4/12/16
5 "District Crime Data at a Glance," Metropolitan Police Department, www.mpdc.dc.gov
6 "Inside the White House: The Hidden Lives of the Modern Presidents and the Secrets of the World's Most Powerful Institution," Ronald Kessler, published 1995
7 "The Un-Civil War: Blacks vs. Niggers," Taleeb Starkes, published 2013
8 "Q&A: Al Sharpton Talks Oscar Boycott, Says African Americans Need to Send Message to Hollywood," variety.com, 1/19/16
9 "Oscars: Al Sharpton Criticizes "Fraudulent" Hollywood Over Zero Nonwhite Acting Noms," hollywoodreporter.com, 1/14/16
10 "Jada Pinkett Smith, Spike Lee to boycott Oscars ceremony," cnn.com, 1/19/16
11 "Jada Pinkett Smith, Spike Lee to boycott Oscars ceremony, cnn.com, 1/19/16
12 "Teen suspect who died after Roswell police chase was heart recipient," ajc.com, 4/1/15
13 "Teen who got heart transplant dies in crash during chase," yahoo.com, 4/1/15
14 "www.blacklivesmatter.com/about/"
15 "Homicide Trends in the United States, 1980-2008," Bureau of Justice Statistics, November 2011
16 "Judge rips thug: 'Black lives don't matter to black people with guns'," nypost.com, 3/29/16
17 "In Ferguson, Jesse Jackson Reportedly Booed After Asking Crowd For Donations," nation.foxnews.com, 8/17/14
18 "Rep. John Lewis: Black Lives Matter Protesters Should Respect Everyone's Right To Be Heard," buzzfeed.com, 10/30/15
19 "The Fierce Urgency of Now: Why Young Protesters Bum-Rushed the Mic," theroot.com, 12/14/14
20 "This Ain't Your Granddaddy's Civil Rights Movement," bet.com, 12/5/14
21 "'Justice for Trayvon' DC: Boycott Disneyland," breitbart.com, 7/20/13
22 "Jesse Jackson suggests boycotting Florida as 'apartheid state'," thehill.com, 7/19/13
23 "Racial Justice," berniesanders.com
24 "Watch: The Black Lives Matter Activist Who Interrupted Hillary Clinton Explains Why," theroot.com, 2/27/16
25 "Early Skirmishes in a Race War," nationalreview.com, 10/24/13
26 "Race War in Obama's America," allenbwest.com, 10/25/13
27 "Jamie Foxx defends 'I kill all the white people' joke," thegrio.com, 12/13/12
28 "Dear White America," nytimes.com, 12/24/15
29 "Protester DeRay Mckesson has moved to STL," stltoday.com, 3/9/15
30 "Ferguson Rent-A-Mobs Exposed," frontpagemag.com, 5/18/15
31 "We Affirm that All Black lives Matter," blacklivesmatter.com/guiding-principles
32 "www.blacklivesmatter.com/find-chapters"
33 "Shooting of Laquan McDonald," wikipedia.org
34 "Police: 2 Shot, 1 Killed In Auburn Gresham," abc7chicago.com, 10/18/15
35 "www.blacklivesmatter.com/about"
36 "15-year-old shot while sleeping was 'loving, bubbly teenager'," wmcactionnews5.com, 4/10/15
37 "'Cowards' Family says 7-year-old was killed in retaliation shooting," wreg.com, 4/23/15
38 "Fiddling Away the Future," creators.com, 7/8/15
39 "Eric H. Holder Jr., in Ferguson, shares painful memories of racism," washingtonpost.com, 8/20/14
40 "Attorney General Eric Holder to students: 'I am also a black man'," msnbc.com 8/20/14
41 "'Urban Militia' Group RbG Black Rebels Offers Bounty For Location Of Officer Darren Wilson," huffingtonpost.com, 11/19/14
42 "What about Jamyla? Lack of activism after Ferguson death draws criticism," rt.com, 8/20/15
43 "Shooting of Tamir Rice," wikipedia.org
44 "Smithsonian Institute seeks to preserve gazebo where Tamir Rice was shot," cleveland.com, 5/2/16
45 "Shooting of Oscar Grant," wikipedia.org
46 "Fruitvale Station," wikipedia.org
47 "www.nabj.org/Constitution"
48 "The Demographics of Social Media Users — 2012," pewinternet.org, 2/14/13
49 "Elderly Couple Sues Spike Lee Over Tweet," thesmokinggun.com, 11/8/13
50 "Homicide Trends in the United States, 1980-2008," Bureau of Justice Statistics, November 2011
51 "Leading Causes of Death by Age Group, Black Males-United States, 2011" www.cdc.gov
52 "Firearm Violence, 1993-2011," www.bjs.gov, May 2013
53 "Lynchings: By State and Race, 1882-1968," www.law2.umkc.edu
54 "2014 Crime in the United States," Expanded Homicide Data Table 1, fbi.gov
55 "Deadliest year in Baltimore history ends with 344 homicides," baltimoresun.com, 1/1/16
56 "Detroit police Chief Craig to gun owners: Defend your homes," clickondetroit.com, 3/7/14

57 "Top 25 Most Dangerous Neighborhoods in America," neighborhoodscout.com
58 "PBMF Statement on WTAE Anchor's Offensive Facebook post," pbmf.org, 3/24/16
59 "'House of horrors' Alleged at Abortion Clinic," nbcnews.com, 1/19/11
60 "Ivy League professor: Award Carson 'coon of the year'," washingtonexaminer.com, 10/6/15
61 "Baltimore won't buy gunshot detection system," baltimoresun.com, 2/7/15
62 "Freddie Gray Empowerment Center opens," wtop.com, 7/11/15
63 "Unrest will cost city $20 million, officials estimate," baltimoresun.com, 5/26/15
64 "Baltimore Mayor: 'Gave Those Who Wished to Destroy Space to Do That'," baltimore.cbslocal.com, 4/25/15
65 "Mosby: Witness Intimidation Needs To End To Stop The Violence," baltimore.cbslocal.com, 8/6/15
66 "Balt. Police Still Trying To Solve McKenzie Elliott's Murder," baltimore.cbslocal.com, 10/13/14
67 "The History of the Congressional Black Caucus (CBC)," https://cbc-butterfield.house.gov/history
68 H.Res.194 - Apologizing for the Enslavement and Racial Segregation of African-Americans, 110th Congress (2007-2008), www.congress.gov
69 "Could Gay Marriage Spur Black Voter Drop?," theroot.com, 9/17/12
70 "Rep. Waters to black voters: 'unleash us' on Obama," thegrio.com, 8/17/11
71 "Could Gay Marriage Spur Black Voter Drop?," theroot.com, 9/17/12
72 "Congresswoman To Black Constituents: "Contain Your Complaining," rebelpundit.com, 9/29/14
73 "Legacy of the Street Administration," 6abc.com, 1/2/08
74 "Among the 10 largest cities, Philly has highest deep-poverty rate," articles.philly.com, 10/1/15
75 "Fiddling Away the Future," creators.com, 7/8/15
76 "Congressional Black Caucus," wikipedia.org
77 "Top 100 Worst Performing Public Schools in the U.S.," neighborhoodscout.com
78 "2 precincts hit hard by Columbus' 2015 homicide toll of 99," dispatch.com, 1/1/16
79 "In 2015, St. Louis Is Headed Toward the Most Homicides in Decades. How Can We Stop The Bloodshed?" riverfronttimes.com, 10/7/15
80 "A Senseless Death" donofalltrades.com, 3/12/15
81 "Murder/Non-negligent Manslaughter, http://cityofflintpd.blogspot.com/
82 "Detroit police say property and violent crime down," freep.com, 1/7/16
83 "Trenton homicides reduced significantly in 2015, but remain high," nj.com, 7/13/15
84 "East Ward Councilwoman on Trenton's gun violence: 'There's a better way'", trenton.homicidewatch.org, 1/21/14
85 "Kelly Report 2014, Gun Violence in America" www.robinkelly.house.gov
86 "#TakingaStand: Mothers of murder victims," wwltv.com, 5/6/16
87 "Top 100 Worst Performing Public Schools in the U.S," neighborhoodscout.com
88 "Officer Beaten by a Convicted Felon Hesitated for Fear of Being Called Racist: Welcome to Post-Ferguson Policing," nationalreview.com, 8/16/15
89 "Philadelphia Police Officers To Hear Message From Mayor Before Hitting The Streets," philadelphia.cbslocal.com, 12/11/14
90 "Philly Police-Involved Shootings Cost Taxpayers Millions," nbcphiladelphia.com, 5/31/13
91 "South Street Gunman Fires At Bystanders, Police Officers," philadelphia.cbslocal.com, 6/2/13
92 "Enough Evidence To Put Two Of Girl's Murder Suspects On Trial," wowt.com, 3/7/14
93 "Chicago's rising gun violence and racial tensions are driving out the wealthy," businessinsider.com, 4/11/16
94 "Police mood appears to hit a low amid fallout from Laquan McDonald video," chicagotribune.com, 2/26/16
95 "FBI Releases 2014 Statistics on Law Enforcement Officers Killed and Assaulted," fbi.gov, 10/19/15
96 "The Myths of Black Lives Matter," wsj.com, 2/11/16
97 "Preliminary Report Concerning February 29, 2016, Officer-Involved Shooting," http://media.graytvinc.com, 3/3/16
98 "Cops are MORE hesitant to shoot armed black suspects than whites, study finds," dailymail.co.uk, 1/6/15
99 "The Engineering of Consent," published 1947, Edward Bernays, web.archive.org
100 "Engaging Diverse Viewpoints: What Is the Campus Climate for Perspective-Taking?" published 2010, www.aacu.org
101 "Treatment of PTSD an Assessment of the Evidence," 2007, www.iom.edu
102 "In Conversation Chris Rock," vulture.com, 11/30/14
103 "Deadliest year in Baltimore history ends with 344 homicides," baltimoresun.com, 1/1/16
104 ""Just Call Them Niggers," Exasperated CNN Guest Tells Erin Burnett," gawker.com, 4/28/15
105 "Grammar snobs are patronising, pretentious and just plain wrong," youtube.com, Mona Chalabi, 4/20/16
106 "Seattle officials call for ban on 'potentially offensive' language," foxnews.com, 8/2/13
107 "PC student tests forbid dance, dinos & lots more," nypost.com, 3/26/12
108 "Everything Is Problematic," University Guide Explains," nymag.com, 7/29/15
109 "Shaky allegations made at March protest on campus," kutower.com, 5/8/15
110 "Message from President Jones Regarding an Incident," albany.edu, 1/30/16

TALEEB STARKES